Stephen U

Stephen Unwin was taught at Cam
Heinemann. Since graduating in 1982, he has directed more than sixty
professional productions, initially at the Traverse Theatre in
Edinburgh, where he was Associate Director. All of his productions
there were new plays from Scotland, England and abroad. Six
transferred to London theatres, including the British premieres of
two plays by Manfred Karge, *Man to Man* and *The Conquest of the
South Pole*. He was resident director at the National Theatre Studio
in the late 1980s.

In 1993, he launched English Touring Theatre. His many productions
for ETT include *Hamlet*, *A Doll's House*, *As You Like It*, *Hedda
Gabler*, *The Taming of the Shrew*, *The Master Builder*, *The Cherry
Orchard*, *Ghosts*, *King Lear*, *John Gabriel Borkman*, *Mother Courage
and Her Children* and *Romeo and Juliet*. His work has been seen at the
Old Vic, the Royal Court, the Donmar and the Lyric Hammersmith.
His other work includes several plays for the Theatre Royal Bath. He
has also directed in repertory theatre and in Europe.

In 2008, he was appointed as Artistic Director of the Rose Theatre
Kingston, where his productions include *The Winslow Boy*, *Hay
Fever*, *The Lady from the Sea*, *The Importance of Being Earnest*, *A Day
in the Death of Joe Egg*, *The Vortex* and *Ghosts*.

He has directed a dozen operas, including the post-war premiere of
Brecht and Eisler's *The Decision*, *The Marriage of Figaro*, *Lucia di
Lammermoor*, *Così fan tutte*, *Gianni Schicchi* (ENO), *Il barbiere di
Siviglia* (ROH), *Albert Herring*, *Falstaff*, *Die Entführung*, *Le nozze di
Figaro*, *Don Giovanni* (Garsington) and *Intermezzo* (Buxton).

He has held numerous academic positions, including a Granada Artist
Professorship at the University of California, the Judith E. Wilson
Visiting Fellowship at Cambridge, and a Halle Distinguished Visiting
Professorship at Emory University in Atlanta, Georgia.

His many books include three *Pocket Guides* for Faber (*Shakespeare*,
Twentieth-Century Drama and *Ibsen, Chekhov and Strindberg*), *So You
Want To Be A Theatre Director?* (Nick Hern Books), *The Well Read
Play* (Oberon) and *A Guide to the Plays of Bertolt Brecht* (Methuen).

The Complete Brecht Toolkit

STEPHEN UNWIN

with Julian Jones

NICK HERN BOOKS
London
www.nickhernbooks.co.uk

A Nick Hern Book

The Complete Brecht Toolkit
first published in Great Britain in 2014
by Nick Hern Books Limited
The Glasshouse, 49a Goldhawk Road, London W12 8QP

Cover designed by Ned Hoste, 2H
Typeset by Nick Hern Books, London
Printed and bound in Great Britain by
Ashford Colour Press Ltd, Gosport, Hampshire

A CIP catalogue record for this book
is available from the British Library

ISBN 978 1 85459 550 8

For our London season we need to bear two things in mind. First: we shall be offering most of the audience a pure pantomime, a kind of silent film on the stage, for they know no German. Second: there is in England a long-standing fear that German art must be terribly heavy, slow, laborious and pedestrian.

So our playing needs to be quick, light, strong. This is not a question of hurry, but of speed, not simply of quick playing, but of quick thinking. We must keep the tempo of a runthrough and infect it with quiet strength, with our own fun. In the dialogue the exchanges must not be offered reluctantly, as when offering somebody one's last pair of boots, but must be tossed like so many balls. The audience has to see that here are a number of artists working together as an ensemble in order to convey stories, ideas, virtuoso feats to the spectator by a common effort.

Good work!

Bertolt Brecht

Brecht's last message to the members of the Berliner Ensemble (5 August 1956). He died nine days later, on 14 August. The Ensemble's London season opened on 27 August, with Mother Courage.

Contents

Acknowledgements

Brecht had dozens of 'collaborators' and – for the most part – acknowledged them. I have fewer, but they deserve credit too.

The late John Willett (1917–2002) recognised that if you have a reasonable grasp of history, a sceptical approach to theory and a robust sense of humour, it's possible to appreciate Brecht's remarkable achievements. I refer to his and Ralph Manheim's (1907–92) editions of the *Collected Works*[1] throughout, as well as to their several volumes of poems,[2] letters,[3] journals,[4] and theatrical theory.[5] Their translations of Brecht have been much criticised but until someone supplants their editions in ways that are true to the plays, in tune with Brecht's intentions and scholarly in their approach, John and Ralph (ably supplemented by Tom Kuhn in recent years) will bear the palm as Brecht's most significant British champions.

The eight volumes of the Methuen *Collected Works* is one of the most lavish compliments paid to a foreign playwright by a British publisher and I'm grateful to Methuen and the Brecht Estate for granting permission to quote from these superb editions. But none of it would have been possible without Nick Hern, the most knowledgeable of theatrical publishers, and long champion of Brecht. His friendship over twenty-five years has meant a great deal to me, and I'm particularly grateful to him for not losing patience with my many delays in delivering this book.

I owe Julian Jones and his excellent students from Rose Bruford College a debt of gratitude for devising the fifty practical exercises in Chapter Five.[6] I'm also fortunate to have worked over the years with hundreds of theatre professionals – actors, directors and others – with whom I've explored the practical application of Brecht's theory.

I especially treasure my collaborations with Tilda Swinton in the 1980s: we tried to understand Brecht's theatre by *doing* it, not by studying the theory. The great Marxist literary critic and teacher Margot Heinemann (1913–92) was our guiding light;[7] but, as Brecht was so fond of quoting, 'The proof of the pudding is in the eating.'

*

The author and publisher acknowledge permission to quote extracts from the following:

Brecht on Theatre © Bertolt Brecht, edited and translated by John Willett. Translation copyright © 1964, renewed 1992 by John Willett. Reprinted by permission of Hill and Wang, a division of Farrar, Straus and Giroux, LLC in the United States of America, and Methuen Drama, an imprint of Bloomsbury Publishing, in the rest of the world.

Collected Plays, Poems, Letters and Journals © Bertolt Brecht. Translated and edited by John Willett, Ralph Manheim and Tom Kuhn. Reprinted by permission of Methuen Drama, an imprint of Bloomsbury Publishing.

1. Methuen have published eight volumes of *The Collected Plays*.
2. *Poems 1913–1956* (1976); *Poems and Songs from the Plays* (1990).
3. *Letters 1913–1956* (1990).
4. *Journals 1934–1956* (1993).
5. *Brecht on Theatre* (1964); *Brecht on Art and Politics* (2003); *Brecht on Film* (2001); and *The Messingkauf Dialogues* (1965).
6. The following graduates from the Rose Bruford Acting and Actor Musician Programmes took part: Dan Dingsdale, Josie Dunn, Maddy Hill, Max Hutchinson, Gill Mackie, Alex Mugnaioni, Kirsty Oswald and Huw Parmentor.
7. In an obituary, Margot Heinemann's lifelong friend and fellow Communist, Eric Hobsbawm, described her as 'one of the most remarkable people of our time and a testament to its indestructible hopes'. I owe many of the insights in this book to her example.

The Complete
Brecht Toolkit

Introduction

Bertolt Brecht (1898–1956) was one of the greatest play-wrights of the twentieth century. He was also a prodigiously talented stage director whose work has had a huge impact on the development of the modern theatre.

His approach is still significant, as the director Peter Brook has acknowledged:

> Brecht is the key figure of our time, and all theatre work today at some point starts or returns to his statements and achievements.[1]

Even in his lifetime, however, Brecht was widely misunderstood. This is partly his own fault: his views were frequently contradictory and he could be wilfully obscure. And he was exceptionally fertile: 'A man with one theory is lost,' he joked. 'He must have several, four, many!' But it's above all because his ideas have been so widely appropriated that it's hard to separate Brecht's own views from those of his later imitators and interpreters.

The aim of this book is to clear away some of the mystery that surrounds Brecht's theatre and explain what he was trying to do. If I express impatience with theory, it's because I subscribe to Brecht's favourite phrase from Hegel: 'The truth is concrete.' And because I know, as a director and teacher, that the best I can offer is rooted in practical experience.

2.

In approaching Brecht, we must be careful to avoid what E.P. Thompson called the 'enormous condescension of posterity'.[2] For Brecht's innovations cannot be understood without a feel – however rudimentary – for the political, social and cultural conditions of his time. We should perhaps bear in mind the following four points:

- Brecht devised his theatrical style as a way of engaging with the world in which he found himself, what he memorably called the 'dark times', and we cannot appreciate the first unless we accept its intimate connection with the second.

- Brecht didn't intend his work to be applicable at all times and places, and refused to set in stone things that were intended to be provisional, and so it's essential that we approach his work historically, as the product of a particular time and place.

- Brecht experimented with many different voices – sometimes mischievous, at other times provocative, and frequently ironic – and it's a mistake to look for a definitive statement of his views; instead, we should assemble our insights from as wide a range of sources as possible.

- Brecht emphasised change, above all: not just the political change that he wanted to bring about, but the great tides of change that make up human history. The world – and the theatre – has changed enormously in the half-century since his death, and any modern understanding of his work must embrace that fact.

In other words, if we are to understand Brecht's theatre, we need to engage with Brecht's unique personality and the very different world in which it emerged. To do anything else would be thoroughly un-Brechtian.

3.

This book was conceived as a partner to the excellent *Complete Stanislavsky Toolkit*.³ But the two figures make uneasy bedfellows. Stanislavsky was a theatre artist, teacher and director, concerned, above all, to make acting a more truthful reflection of observable reality. Brecht, by contrast, was a highly political figure dedicated to creating a kind of theatre that could engage audiences in a critical dialogue about society. Stanislavsky was interested in the theatre; for Brecht, the world beyond the stage door came first.

Sadly, Brecht is often sloppily taught, and his self-conscious style is regarded as theatricality for its own sake. Indeed, his contemporaries criticised him for the same 'formalism': an interest in art for its formal properties and not for its success in depicting human experience. But Brecht was forthright about the relationship between the stage and the world:

> The modern theatre mustn't be judged by its success in satisfying the audience's habits but by its success in transforming them. It needs to be questioned not about its degree of conformity with the 'eternal laws of the theatre' but about its ability to master the rules governing the great social processes of our age; not about whether it manages to interest the spectator in buying a ticket – i.e. in the theatre itself – but about whether it manages to interest him in the world.⁴

In other words, like Hamlet, Brecht didn't just want his theatre to 'hold the mirror up to nature', he insisted that it should 'show virtue her own feature, scorn her own image, and the very age and body of the time his form and pressure'.⁵ Adapting a famous phrase from Karl Marx, he declared that 'the theatre has hitherto interpreted the world, the point is to change it',⁶ and this central imperative ('Change the world, it needs it!'⁷) runs through all of his work.

Brecht set out his astonishingly ambitious intentions in his twenties:

It is understood that the *radical transformation of the theatre* can't be the result of some artistic whim. It has simply to correspond to the whole radical transformation of the mentality of our time.[8]

And so our exploration of Brecht's theatrical techniques needs to recognise, above all, the relationship between theatrical form and the rapidly changing world beyond.

4.

Brecht can be daunting. At its best, however, his theatre is based on tremendous simplicity: not a simplicity that fails to tell the truth, but an approach to theatre – and writing – that expresses what really matters:

> And I always thought: the very simplest words
> Must be enough. When I say what things are like
> Everyone's heart must be torn to shreds.
> That you'll go down if you don't stand up for yourself
> Surely you see that.[9]

With its passion and its rage, its confidence and its scepticism, its elegance and its concision, this last poem is a guiding light for anyone interested in the challenge that Brecht sets us. It should be pinned up in any room where his fascinating, challenging and occasionally bewildering theatre is being explored.

1. Peter Brook, *The Empty Space* (1969).
2. E.P. Thompson, *The Making of the English Working Class* (1963).
3. Bella Merlin, *The Complete Stanislavsky Toolkit* (2007).
4. 'A Little Private Tuition for my Friend Max Gorelik' (1944).
5. *Hamlet*, 3.2.
6. Karl Marx, *Theses on Feurbach* (1845): 'Philosophers have hitherto only interpreted the world in various ways; the point is to change it.'
7. *The Decision.*
8. 'The Epic Theatre and its Difficulties' (1927).
9. 'And I Always Thought', *Poems 1913–1956.*

I

In Context

I

In Context

BRECHT: A LIFE IN THEATRE

'May you live in interesting times,'[1] runs the ancient Chinese curse. Brecht's life coincides with the most 'interesting' half-century in European history and a series of linked catastrophes – the Great War, the Russian Revolution, the Great Depression, the rise of Fascism, the Second World War and the division of Germany – shaped his writing in ways that are unimaginable to 'those born later'.[2]

Brecht's story has been frequently told, sometimes at length, in several critical studies and biographies.[3] These usually focus on his development as a dramatist, poet and political thinker – with his colourful private life making an occasional appearance[4] – but with little insight into his practical work in the theatre, or the evolution of his theatrical theory.[5] What follows, then, is an attempt to chart Brecht's development into the most influential stage director and theatrical innovator of the twentieth century.

Bavaria: 1898–1923

Brecht was born into a middle-class family in the sleepy Bavarian city of Augsburg. He spent much of his youth in an apolitical reverie, chasing girls, writing Expressionist poetry, running a puppet theatre and entertaining his friends by gruffly singing songs to a guitar. He attended a decent school, studied medicine in nearby Munich, and worked for a short while as a hospital orderly in the chaos following Germany's surrender in the First World War.

Munich was a melting pot. Although it was to become noto-
rious as the home of the Nazis, it boasted a rich left-wing
tradition and, along with Berlin and Vienna, was one of the great
cultural centres of the German-speaking world. Brecht served
briefly as an Independent Socialist on the Workers' Council
there and witnessed the failed 'Spartacist' revolution at first
hand. He attended the drama seminars of the legendary Arthur
Kutscher, wrote pieces of theatre criticism and played a small
part in the political cabarets of Karl Valentin. He left university
without a degree and soon fathered two illegitimate children.
And he started to write plays.

In 1921, Brecht went to Berlin with the aim of breaking into
the theatre as a director. He quickly got to know many of the
leading theatrical figures and touted for work. He secured his
first production, Arnolt Bronnen's *Parricide*, but fought so badly
with the leading actors that he was eventually sacked, gaining
an early – if almost certainly deserved – reputation for being
'difficult'. Undaunted, he was appointed dramaturg (literary
manager) at the Kammerspiele in Munich, where his second
play, *Drums in the Night*, was premiered. The production was
entrusted to an inexperienced young director, but Brecht
attended rehearsals and shaped the result; when staged in the
capital a few months later, he assumed all directorial
responsibility.

In May 1923, Erich Engel, who was to become one of his
closest 'collaborators', directed Brecht's third play, *In the Jungle
of the Cities*. His old school friend, Caspar Neher ('Cas'), was
responsible for the set designs but, again, Brecht interfered with
every aspect of the production, which was greeted with howls
of derision. When, later the same year, Brecht co-directed a
minor Expressionist piece about adolescence, its author was so
dismayed that he got the production closed. In December,
Brecht's first play, *Baal*, received its belated premiere in
Leipzig: nominally directed by another director, once again
Brecht made all the most important decisions. And, predictably,
both play and production were slated.

Brecht's fortunes changed in 1924. His (and Lion Feucht-wanger's) adaptation of Marlowe's *Edward II* was a critical hit, and gave an early indication of the amazing theatrical techniques that characterise his mature work. And, as a result, Brecht was able to call himself a director in his own right.

Berlin: 1924–33

Brecht moved to Berlin in 1924 where he married the young Austrian actress, Helene Weigel, who soon bore him two children (Stefan and Barbara). His colourful private life – he had dozens of lovers – has provoked much comment, but the long-suffering Weigel didn't just give him the stability he needed to work, she created many of his greatest roles. He also met the Anglo-American scholar Elisabeth Hauptmann who provided him with intellectual challenge, secretarial support and literary advice for the rest of his life. The plain fact is that Brecht couldn't have achieved half of what he did without the support of these two remarkable women.

The German capital was enjoying an extraordinary renais-sance. This was the Berlin of Auden and Isherwood, George Grosz and Otto Dix, the Kroll Opera and political cabaret, as well as feminism, sexual liberation and alternative lifestyles. It was also home to a feast of radical theatre, with great directors such as Erwin Piscator, Leopold Jessner and Max Reinhardt all producing work that made a decisive break with naturalism. What's more, the city hosted visiting companies from around the world, including astonishing productions by Vsevolod Mey-erhold, Sergei Eisenstein and others from the new Soviet Union. With its explosive mix of political upheaval and cultural radicalism, it provided the ideal climate for Brecht's pugnacious theatrical personality to flourish.

Brecht was a founding member of 'Group 1925', a group of nearly forty poets, novelists and dramatists committed to the radicalisation of German culture. In 1926, he co-directed a revival of *Baal*; designed by Neher, with the extraordinary

Oskar Homolka playing the title role, this had only a single performance but gave further indications of Brecht's emerging
genius. And 1926 saw simultaneous premieres of the key tran-
sitional piece, *Man Equals Man*: a flop in Düsseldorf, it was a
succès de scandale in Darmstadt.

In 1927, Brecht directed the first of his collaborations with
Kurt Weill, *The Mahagonny Songspiel*, at the avant-garde Baden-
Baden Music Festival. He had become a member of the
'dramaturgical collective' at the Volksbühne, where Piscator's
production of *The Good Soldier Schweik*, designed by Grosz,
had made a huge impact. And, finally, the triumphant – if
scratch – production of *The Threepenny Opera* became Brecht's
greatest hit and gave him unprecedented influence and
independence.

Meanwhile, over-dependent on US bonds, the modest German economic recovery was stopped in its tracks by the Wall
Street Crash, and Brecht witnessed the poverty and social chaos
that resulted. Although he never joined the Communist Party,
his work as writer and director should be seen within the context of the broad movement against capitalism, whose failure, it
maintained, was causing the injustice evident all around. Brecht
started to read Karl Marx and dedicated himself to creating a
kind of theatre that could not just interpret the world, but help
to change it.

Brecht's friendship with the socialist intellectual Walter Benjamin helped him clarify his views of the relationship between
aesthetics and politics,[6] and he soon started to articulate his proposals for a new kind of theatre suitable for the new world.[7] He
co-directed two plays by the young Marieluise Fleisser and premiered the first of his 'learning plays' (the *Lehrstücke*). And
exactly a year after *The Threepenny Opera*, he co-directed, again
with Engel, the premiere of his and Hauptmann's *Happy End*.
But this was a tremendous flop and it – along with Nazi thugs
protesting the premiere of *The Rise and Fall of the City of
Mahagonny* – marked the end of the happy-go-lucky days of the
Weimar Republic.

In 1930, the Romanian director Slatan Dudow premiered
Brecht's politically explosive learning play *The Decision* (sometimes known as *The Measures Taken*). The following year Brecht
directed his own astonishing production of *Man Equals Man*,
described by Sergei Tretyakov in vivid terms:

> Giant soldiers armed to the teeth and wearing jackets
> caked with lime, blood and excrement stalk about the
> stage, holding on to wires to keep from falling off stilts
> inside their trouser legs.

Not until *Mother Courage* would he create such an overwhelming theatrical event, and it provided a template for much of his
subsequent development.

In 1932, Brecht met – and fell in love with – the young
working-class intellectual, Margarete Steffin. His last theatrical
venture in Weimar Germany was his own razor-sharp adaptation
of Maxim Gorky's *The Mother*, seen first at the Theater am
Schiffbauerdamm, and then in working-class districts across
Berlin. This, along with *The Decision*, cemented Brecht's
position as the pre-eminent left-wing dramatist in the world.

While Brecht had become increasingly drawn to Communism, huge numbers of his fellow Germans embraced National
Socialism. With the appointment of Hitler as Chancellor in January 1933, Brecht's work was immediately banned. One of the
world's most sophisticated societies was sinking into barbarism
and Brecht fled into exile.

Scandinavia: 1933–41

Brecht went first to Vienna, and then Zurich and Paris, where
he attended rehearsals for his and Weill's ballet, *The Seven
Deadly Sins*. He eventually joined his family – and Steffin – in
Denmark, where he met the talented but troubled photographer
and actress Ruth Berlau.

Brecht's eight years in Scandinavia were characterised by
enormous creativity, not just in playwriting, but also in the

development of his theatrical theory. He wrote dozens of essays, letters and articles, and started to keep his astonishing *Journal*. He received many eminent visitors, and it was there that he did the most productive thinking about a theatre that could make a contribution to the all-important goal of defeating Fascism.

In terms of practical work, however, Brecht was forced to rely on the amateur theatre. He oversaw – and interfered with – amateur Danish productions of *The Mother*, *Round Heads and Pointed Heads* and *The Seven Deadly Sins*, and travelled first to Moscow and then New York, to attend the US premiere of *The Mother*. But there were no opportunities for the professional directing that he had started to enjoy in Berlin.

Dudow directed the Paris premiere of Brecht's one-act Spanish Civil War drama, *Señora Carrar's Rifles* in late 1937, and December saw its Danish premiere. The following year, Dudow directed eight scenes of *Fear and Misery of the Third Reich*, with Weigel as the Jewish Wife. With Hitler's armies threatening Denmark, Brecht and his entourage moved on to Sweden, where he wrote his anti-war masterpiece, *Mother Courage and Her Children*.

In 1940, Brecht moved to Finland, where he wrote perhaps his most important theoretical work, *The Messingkauf Dialogues*; he also sketched out *The Good Person of Szechwan* and wrote his comic parable *Mr Puntila and his Man Matti*. Finally, with most of Europe under Nazi rule, Brecht's party left for Moscow, where Steffin died of tuberculosis. With Weigel, Berlau and the two children, he made his way to Vladivostok and boarded a ship for Los Angeles.

USA: 1941–47

Although Brecht's years in America were exceptionally productive for the playwright – he completed many of his finest plays there, including *The Good Person of Szechwan*, *The Resistible Rise of Arturo Ui*, *Schweik in the Second World War*, *The Caucasian Chalk Circle* and *Life of Galileo* – they were deeply frustrating for the director. He found it almost impossible to make headway in Hollywood and there was no demand for German-speaking theatre in America. And, although *Mother Courage* was premiered in neutral Switzerland in 1941, Brecht was unable to see it. At times, he must have wondered whether he would ever direct again.

Apart from overseeing the American premiere of *Fears and Miseries*, Brecht's theatrical work was confined to an unsuccessful adaptation (with W.H. Auden) of Webster's *The Duchess of Malfi*, and his translation with Charles Laughton of *Galileo*. This bore fruit in 1947, with Brecht's formidable American production of the play first in Los Angeles and then in New York. But, for the most part, Brecht was a fish out of water during his six long years in the USA.

East Berlin: 1948–56

America, however, gave Brecht the space to hone his ideas for his triumphant return to Europe.

Having mystified the House Un-American Activities Committee, Brecht went to Switzerland, the only country in Europe that had produced his work during the war. His radical adaptation in February 1948 of Sophocles' *Antigone* in the small Swiss town of Chur gave an early indication of his mature theatrical style. He co-directed the premiere of *Puntila* in Zurich and wrote *A Short Organum for the Theatre*, one of his most important pieces of theatrical theory. He also met up with old friends and colleagues – often after a gap of fifteen traumatic years – and made plans for the future.

Brecht finally arrived in the ruins of East Berlin in October 1948, and set about preparing his magnificent production of *Mother Courage*: with Weigel in the title role, this received its premiere in the war-damaged Deutsches Theater in January 1949. As a result of its huge success, Brecht and Weigel secured funds for a new company, the Berliner Ensemble, with Weigel as Intendant (Chief Executive) and Brecht as Artistic Director. For the first time, Brecht, aged fifty-one, had access to a theatre where he could direct his plays and put his many ideas into practice.

The Ensemble's first production was *Puntila*: co-directed with Engel, this opened in November 1949. In spring 1950, Brecht's adaptation of *The Tutor* was premiered and, in October, he directed a new production of *Mother Courage* in Munich with Therese Giehse – who had first created it in Zurich – in the title role. And all the time he was gathering around him some of the finest – and most politically committed – of German actors and theatre artists.

In 1951, Brecht directed *The Mother* with Weigel in the role she had first played before the war. But the authorities disapproved of his and Eisler's opera, *The Trial of Lucullus*; extensively rewritten as *The Condemnation of Lucullus*, it was finally premiered in October. The next year, Brecht started work on an adaptation of Shakespeare's *Coriolanus* and, in November, oversaw a revival of *Señora Carrar's Rifles*. 1953 was a difficult year for Brecht: his refusal to condemn the violent suppression of a working-class uprising exposed him to the charge of supporting the increasingly repressive East German state. Moving inwards, he wrote a fine – if melancholic – collection of poems, *The Buckow Elegies*.

Perhaps in gratitude for Brecht's silence, the Berliner Ensemble was given the Theater am Schiffbauerdamm – where *The Threepenny Opera* had been premiered twenty-six years previously – as its permanent home. Brecht launched its residence there with his astonishing production of *The Caucasian Chalk Circle*. Brilliantly designed by Karl von Appen, this – along with *Mother Courage* and *Galileo* – was one of the defining works of Brecht's theatrical reputation.

The following year, *Mother Courage* visited Paris and its huge impact helped secure Brecht's international reputation. In 1955, he started work on a new production of *Galileo* with Ernst Busch, his old comrade from the 1930s, in the title role. The Ensemble made its second visit to Paris and, in 1956, appeared at the London World Theatre Season. But Brecht was too ill to travel and he died in Berlin on 14 August 1956.

THE ROOTS OF BRECHT'S THEATRE

Brecht's theatre had many fathers: 'Shakespeare?' he liked to boast. 'He was a thief too...'[8] He had a magpie's ability to find inspiration in almost everything he encountered – from great classical art to the most raucous of popular entertainment – and when exploring his theatrical innovations we should remember the many writers and literary styles that helped to shape them.

The Bible

Brecht's lifelong interest in the Bible may come as a surprise to the student of the radical playwright. But while Brecht shared the usual left-wing suspicion of religion – 'the opium of the masses' as Marx called it[9] – he knew that a writer interested in the poor and the powerless needed to harness its huge charge. Indeed, when asked by a women's magazine which book had influenced him most, he replied, 'The Bible. Don't laugh...'

Brecht's early plays – *Baal, Drums in the Night, Man Equals Man* and *Saint Joan of the Stockyards* – often show ordinary people crucified by a cruel system. A more nuanced reading of the Bible is evident in the 'epic' plays – especially *Mother Courage, Szechwan, Galileo* and *The Caucasian Chalk Circle* – whose individual episodes are designed to make a particular point, and whose action is endowed with pedagogic meaning. As with the Bible, they constantly make us aware of their intentions, however sophisticated.

The Bible's emphasis on ordinary people offered Brecht a sense of how to combine the ordinary with the sublime, the earthy with the grand, and the pragmatic with the visionary. He especially admired the parables of the New Testament, whose concision, elegance and boldness gave him a model for a new kind of political theatre, which communicated its points through graphic *exempla*. Brecht grasped that they show change and development through a series of gestural actions: instead of trying to explain causality through psychological or social analysis, they declare 'this happened and then that happened', and leave us to come to our own conclusions.

Brecht wanted to achieve a similar simplicity. His productions concentrated, above all, on the human figure and a few telling objects, set against an empty background and under brilliant light. And he used short dramatisations of episodes from the Bible in his actor training. Brecht hoped that this emphasis on pure action, unmediated by morality or explanation, would guide the audience inexorably towards the play's pedagogical purpose, event after event, action by action, moment by moment.

The Bible is less resonant today than it was to Brecht's contemporaries. But its simple narrative style is as compelling as ever, and we in the secular modern theatre can learn much from Brecht's cunning appropriation of its dramatic power.

▶ See Exercises 7, 8, 9, 10, 11 & 12[10]

Aristotle

Most theories of drama start with a reading of Aristotle's *Poetics*.[11] This slim volume of lecture notes had a huge impact on eighteenth- and nineteenth-century theories of *mimesis*, especially in Germany and France, where literary critics emphasised a unified narrative structure and spoke of the dual sensations of 'pity and terror' which, through a process of 'empathy', produced feelings of 'catharsis' in the audience.

Brecht based many of his proposals for a new kind of theatre on an explicit rejection of *The Poetics*. He dismissed 'empathy' as an evasion of critical engagement and maintained that the 'unities' (the action should take place in one location, with a consistent *dramatis personae* and over the course of a single day) produced drama incapable of representing the contradictory textures of the modern world.

This rejection of Aristotle encourages us to seek out tonal contrasts and avoid the kind of homogeneity that neoclassical dramatic rules so readily produce. More importantly, it helps us stage drama with a more sceptical – above all, more objective –

approach to the experiences of the central characters, and reminds us of the limitations of 'empathy' as the chief goal of the theatre.

But, as ever, Brecht's critique needs to be placed within its historical cultural context. In confronting Aristotle, he was addressing his contemporaries as much as the Greek philosopher himself. As Margot Heinemann points out, 'Brecht's deep hostility to *Einfühlung*, total emotional identification as the main basis of performance, can't be seen as purely an aesthetic preference; it is historical and political'. Brecht himself argued:

> Already in the last years of the Weimar Republic, the
> German drama took a decisively rationalistic turn.
> Fascism's grotesque emphasising of the emotions, and
> perhaps no less a certain decline of the rational element
> in Marxist teaching, led me personally to lay particular
> stress on the rational.[12]

What's more, Brecht read *The Poetics* selectively. He ignored Aristotle's emphasis on the story and failed to recognise that thought and dramatic irony limit – and occasionally deny – empathy. And, as he came to recognise, Aristotle's arguments, especially the 'unities', have been more influential in French and German theatre than in Britain, where Shakespeare's informality has dominated. What Brecht was really doing was rejecting 'the well-made play' – a kind of bourgeois drama he despised – and the histrionic and overemotional acting that was dominant in the German theatre of his time.

▸ See Exercises 7, 8, 9, 10, 11 & 12 (Story and Narrative)
   and 13, 14, 15, 16, 17 & 18 (Argument and Clarity)

The Classical World

Brecht was fascinated by the writers of Ancient Rome, who provided him with a model of a sophisticated, market-driven, class-divided society, unimpeded by the moralising so common in Christianity.

Four writers were particularly important: Tacitus' flinty, unadorned style offered him a template of clarity in political discussion and Horace's stoical materialism was especially congenial, while the urban comedies of Plautus and the political tragedies of Seneca gave him prototypes for his dramatisations of the amoral drives that shape the modern world.

This fascination bore fruit in several minor works: the learning play *The Horatians and Curatians*, the abandoned novel *The Business Affairs of Mr Julius Caesar* and the opera *The Trial* (later *Condemnation*) *of Lucullus*; but it's most spectacularly on display in Brecht's reworking of Shakespeare's *Coriolanus*, which offered him the broadest canvas on which to develop his concerns about the distribution of power and wealth.

Classical Greece gave Brecht less to get his teeth into. He read various Greek poets and wrote a philosophical poem in homage to Empedocles' shoe.[13] But his most significant engagement was his adaptation of Sophocles' *Antigone*, which combined a modern prologue – set in the ruins of bombed-out Berlin – with a powerful projection of the original as a parable of tyranny and resistance, setting Creon's dictatorship against Antigone's rebellious, heroic individualism.

Brecht's preoccupations should be distinguished from high modernism's appropriation of the classical world. Whereas James Joyce and T.S. Eliot used it to imply continuity in human experience, Brecht was drawn to its ability to portray social and political processes realistically and objectively. In other words, the classical world appealed to Brecht because of its particularity, not its universality.

An understanding of Brecht's classical interests – like his fascination with the Bible – should help us see how a radical artist can build on the foundations of western culture to create cutting-edge art for our time. In other words, modernity has many fathers.

▶ See Exercises 13, 15, 15, 16, 17 & 18 (Argument and Clarity)[14]

The Oriental Theatre

Like many of his contemporaries, the young Brecht was attracted by a crude westernised version of oriental culture, which offered a wide repertoire of characters and dramatic situations: the brutal 'inscrutability' of the Malayan lumber-dealer Schlink in *In the Jungle of the Cities* or the Sacristan Wang in *Man Equals Man* gave him colourful – if sometimes stereotypical – forces for his dramatisation of the dog-eat-dog violence of the modern world.

In time, however, he developed a more refined approach. Elisabeth Hauptmann introduced him to Arthur Waley's translations of ancient Chinese and Japanese plays, whose intellectual clarity and theatrical simplicity enthralled him. He was especially struck by their dispensing of illusion and realised that, as with the Elizabethans, oriental theatre relies on the audience's imagination. This is the central formal influence behind the 'learning plays': the finest, *The Decision*, takes the form of a report given by four Communist agitators travelling into pre-revolutionary China, and combines traditional theatrical techniques with all the paraphernalia of the modern industrialised world.

Brecht returned to oriental models in exile, but in a less self-conscious fashion. He had been profoundly affected by the Chinese theatre and in *The Good Person of Szechwan* used a recognisably contemporary setting to dramatise the deformities inflicted by capitalism. And *The Caucasian Chalk Circle* borrows oriental elements – the mimed bridge, the use of masks, and so on – to tell its parable of property and ownership.

Brecht's appropriation of oriental theatre treads a fine line. At its best, it helped him create a highly sophisticated, anti-illusionist modernity. But in his notes to *Szechwan*, he voiced his concerns about 'chinoiserie', a kind of cultural imperialism he hated.[15] In his last years, increasingly sensitive to the issue, he confined his interests to an (unsuccessful) adaptation of *Turandot*, and a series of meditations on the ancient Chinese philosopher Lao Tzu.

Brecht's approach should be distinguished from the assimilation of oriental theatre evident in the work of Ariane Mnouchkine or Peter Brook. It had its own distinctly western purpose: a dramatic style of clarity, delicacy and elegance, which provoked the audience into comment on what was being shown, and dissected the modern world even as it presented it. It's still useful today, even if we need to be more wary than ever of 'orientalism'.[16]

Shakespeare and his Contemporaries

Like most Germans of his generation, Brecht first encountered Shakespeare through the filter of Romanticism, with its emphasis on the noble individual standing aloof from society, and was suspicious as a result. But he came to identify Shakespeare as the great dramatist of a changing world – from the feudal to the modern, the medieval to the renaissance, the monarchical to the republican – and recognised that his plays are theatrically gripping, rich with human detail and politically coherent. He was, above all, drawn to the fluidity of Shakespeare's theatrical style, moving from place to place and across classes and worlds; indeed it could be argued that everything that is meant by his theatrical practice can be found in Shakespeare, and that Brecht's chief achievement was to adapt Shakespeare's dramatic style for the modern world.

Brecht's fascination is evident in many of his poems, letters and diary entries. It can be seen in his youthful adaptation of Christopher Marlowe's *Edward II*. More significant was his use of Elizabethan parody to tell the story of Hitler's rise to power in *Arturo Ui*. He cheerfully admitted to stealing from Shakespeare, even declaring that Shakespeare wrote for 'a theatre full of alienation effects!' But throughout his life we can sense Brecht struggling with this drama, admiring its technical skill while also dismissing its content as irrelevant. Perhaps most remarkable of all was his comprehensive reworking of *Coriolanus*. But it's telling that only a year before he died, Brecht admitted, grudgingly, that it would be 'possible to stage *Coriolanus* as it is, with good direction'.[17]

Brecht's most important statements on Shakespeare can be found in the imaginary conversation between a Dramaturg, a Philosopher, an Actor and others, known as *The Messingkauf Dialogues*. In it he proposes two apparently mutually exclusive approaches. On the one hand, he argues, the plays should be regarded historically, as the product of an alien world, 'drama for cannibals', as he mischievously called them; on the other, they should be ransacked for their contemporary energies and changed to serve the purposes of the modern theatre. The tension between these two positions runs through his entire engagement with Shakespeare.

This will be explored in more detail later (see *Brecht on Shakespeare* below): for now we should remember that Shakespeare is the single most significant influence on the evolution of Brecht's theatre and that many of the things we take for granted in the modern way of presenting Shakespeare – the importance of the narrative, the rapidly shifting locations, the free and easy relationship with the audience and the robust acceptance of the limits of illusion – are a direct result of Brecht's remarkably acute insights into his great predecessor.

▶ See Exercises 1, 2, 3, 4, 5 & 6 (The Ensemble)

European Classical Drama

If Brecht's study of Shakespearean drama was decisive, he had an easier – if less enthusiastic – relationship with eighteenth- and early nineteenth-century theatre.

Inevitably, the great trio of German Romantic dramatists influenced him enormously. Goethe, the most philosophical of the three, had the least impact on Brecht, who staged his own reworking of the fragmentary *Urfaust* (1772–75) but showed little interest otherwise. Schiller was the most political and dramatised the struggle against despotism brilliantly: his influence on Brecht is especially evident in the way he made each

scene rehearse a particular argument and never allowed the audience to forget the playwright's controlling intelligence. But it was
the neurotic radical Heinrich von Kleist whom Brecht found the
most sympathetic: he admired *The Broken Jug* (1806) with its
peasant realism and poetic conception, drew on the corrupt
Judge Adam in creating Azdak in the *Chalk Circle*, and oversaw
a production of the play at the Ensemble in the 1950s; and he was
fascinated by *The Prince of Homburg* (1809–10), Kleist's tragic
masterpiece, and wrote a sonnet in response to its troubling
political implications.[18] But, significantly, he also declared himself frustrated by the closed perfection of Kleist's style.

Other eighteenth-century German playwrights include Jakob
Lenz, whose *The Tutor* (1774) Brecht adapted and directed at
the Ensemble, and Gotthold Ephraim Lessing, whose *Hamburg
Dramaturgy* (1767–70) provided him with a template for a discussion of all things theatrical. The most influential, however,
was Georg Büchner, whose fragmentary tragedy of the common
man, *Woyzeck* (1836), prefigures Brecht in the rawness of its
subject matter, the poetic edginess of its language, and the force
of its theatrical impact.[19]

Brecht was fascinated by English literature, especially
eighteenth-century English drama. With the help of Elisabeth
Hauptmann, he plundered Gay's *The Beggar's Opera* (1728) for
The Threepenny Opera, and adapted Farquhar's *The Recruiting
Officer* (1706) as *Trumpets and Drums*. It was English drama's
materialism that appealed to him most. Although he doesn't
refer to Dr Johnson directly, one can imagine him enjoying his
robust pragmatism in matters aesthetic, even if he would have
been dismayed by his political conservatism.

French neoclassical theatre was different. Its assimilation of
the Italian popular tradition helped Brecht detect its radical
streak but, for the most part, he found it too light, too aesthetic
for his purposes. The notable exception was Molière, whose great
comedies satirise power and society in a way that Brecht found
especially congenial. He co-directed his own adaptation of *Dom
Juan* and refers to Molière frequently in his theoretical work.

Brecht understood that the modern bourgeoisie burst its way onto 'the stage of history' – as it's sometimes described in Marxist jargon – with exceptional *élan*. One might presume that Brecht would dismiss the 'middle-class' revolutions; instead, he recognised that the conflicts and energies of these years created the modern world and that its culture should not be ignored. The sophistication of this material is fundamental to Brecht's mature style – and is often overlooked.

Naturalism

Émile Zola declared that 'there is more poetry in the little apartment of a bourgeois than in all the empty, worm-eaten palaces of history'.[20] Naturalism, the movement that he launched, argued that the everyday – money and work, food and drink, marriage and divorce, childbirth and death – were all suitable subjects of art, which could describe reality with the same level of objectivity that was being achieved in science. The naturalists argued that an individual's actions were the product of his environment, and saw the study of the material surfaces of the world as essential. This had enduring consequences on all those who followed, and Brecht's work – so often thought of as the antithesis of naturalism – was impossible without its pioneering achievements.

Brecht, of course, had a complex relationship with naturalism, and his reaction against it needs to be seen as a rejection of its subject – bourgeois life – rather than as a disapproval of its artistic form. Although he showed little interest in the great trio of naturalistic playwrights (Ibsen, Chekhov and Strindberg), he recognised the political radicalism of Hauptmann, Bernard Shaw and Sean O'Casey.[21] What's more, his plays are frequently more naturalistic than imagined: perhaps the most strictly naturalistic were his great cycle of plays about the early years of Nazi rule, *Fears and Misery*, *Señora Carrar's Rifles*, and his final masterpiece, *The Days of the Commune*. And the fundamentals of naturalism can be seen in many of the epic dramas on which his reputation is built.

The crucial point is that Brecht had little objection to naturalism as such, but insisted that the subject of that naturalism should be seen as capable of being changed. As a resolute materialist he knew that the things of the world – food, shelter, clothes, houses, water, etc. – have a fundamental affect on character. His crucial innovation was to present three-dimensional action in discrete sections, set in dramatic juxtaposition against each other, so that broader connections can be made. In other words, he wanted naturalistic effects to play their part in a more dynamic analysis of the way that the world works.

Stanislavsky – the chief practical exponent of naturalism in the theatre – is often regarded as antithetical to Brecht. Certainly, Brecht's early work consciously rejects him and his plays eschew fixed Stanislavskian notions of character. But not only did Brecht recognise the fundamental strengths of Stanislavsky's achievements,[22] his mature work draws on many of the same key elements in his approach to acting: class, age, environment, objective, obstacle, and so on.

Intriguingly, in 1936, Brecht worked for a few days in New York with the father of the American Method School, Lee Strasberg, on Brecht's most explicitly didactic and anti-illusionist piece, *The Decision*. He broke off because of 'political reasons': 'It is a great pity,' Brecht wrote to Strasberg, 'because I had the impression that we worked very well together'.[23] In other words, the differences between Brecht, Stanislavsky and the Method School have been overstated and naturalism is less alien to Brecht than the simple antithesis suggests. We need to disentangle the two traditions with care.

▶ See Exercise 40 (Internal Soundtrack)

Nineteenth-century Literature

If Brecht's relationship to naturalism was complex, his rejection of the bourgeois certainties of much *belle époque* culture was much more clear-cut.

As a young man, however, Brecht was drawn to the work of three French visionaries: Rimbaud, Verlaine and Baudelaire, whose poetry offered hugely sensual accounts of the loner in the busy city, and gave him powerful prototypes for his dreamers alienated from the society in which they found themselves.

Another unlikely fascination was Kipling, the great poet of the British Empire, whose empathy for the common soldier appealed to Brecht's interest in politics 'from the bottom up'. This is most in evidence in *Man Equals Man*, a militaristic fantasy set in British India, but can also be found in *The Threepenny Opera* (especially the carnivorous Tiger Brown) and the cheerful brutality of the soldiers in *Mother Courage*. Willett draws attention to a fascinating prophecy by Kipling that looks forward to Brecht himself:

> But it will take a more mighty intellect to write the Songs of the People. Some day a man will rise up from Bermondsey, Battersea or Bow and he will be coarse but clear-sighted, hard but infinitely and tenderly humorous, speaking the people's tongue, steeped in their lives and telling them in swinging, urging, dinging verse what it is that their inarticulate lips would express.[24]

Once again, we should remember that Brecht's approach is hardly narrow-minded: he stole from everywhere, even the Imperialist enemy.

Popular Culture

Brecht was fascinated by all kinds of popular culture: he loved the Bavarian fairs with their ballad singers and performing monkeys, enjoyed popular music, read Karl May, Jack London and Upton Sinclair, and devoured detective stories. He was both attracted and repelled by Hollywood and tried – without much success – to resolve the contradiction between its robust populism and what he called the 'narcotic' quality of many of its products.

Brecht drew two key lessons from popular culture. The first was its emphasis on the story, at the expense of almost everything else; the second was its readiness to dispense with verisimilitude or psychological credibility if it got in the way of entertainment (or message). He looked to popular culture for liberation from the narrowly aesthetic constraints of the bourgeois theatre.

But popular art confronted Brecht with a familiar problem. On the one hand, he knew that only the greatest is good enough for the working class; on the other, he recognised that classical culture has often excluded the poor and the downtrodden, and left huge areas of human experience unrepresented. How to resolve these questions is the chief stumbling block in discussions about the role of art in revolutionary politics, and Brecht played an important role in helping to shape the terms of this knotty debate.

Popular culture plays a different role today. The commercial is often granted artistic respectability and it's difficult for modern theatre artists to claim the popular as an instrument of radical subversion or political questioning. And in a time when the serious and challenging is often dismissed as elitist, we need to approach Brecht's championing of the radical potential of popular culture with care. But nor should we forget that he wanted, above all, to create a kind of theatre that could strike a chord among ordinary working people.[25]

Peasant Art

Like many on the left, Brecht had a contradictory attitude towards the peasantry. While he knew that they played a key role in creating a new society and believed that only an alliance of the proletariat and the peasantry could spark a successful revolution, he was sceptical about the conservative tendencies of the people who live off the land. Marx and Engels had spoken dismissively in *The Communist Manifesto* of the 'idiocy of rural life', and Brecht shared many of the same prejudices.

This can be seen in Brecht's attitude to folk art. While he accepted that a progressive theatre should draw on its resources, he knew that he was in competition with totalitarian regimes that had assimilated it for their own repulsive ends. Hitler celebrated the 'timeless wisdom' of the German *Volk*, and Stalin did something similar.[26] He knew that the 'people' is a word that needs to be used with care.

Inevitably, Brecht's attitudes changed: in *The Mother*, the peasants take time to recognise the value of the proletariat in their struggle with the landowners and, in *Señora Carrar's Rifles*, a peasant woman's caution is challenged by her actual experience of Fascism. Brecht's mature plays have more complex portraits: in *Puntila* we encounter peasants caught between supporting the revolution and serving the landowners, and in *Mother Courage* they are seen as capable of narrow-minded short-termism and envious brutality, while also playing an important role in exposing the injustices of the world.

The Caucasian Chalk Circle offers some of Brecht's most enjoyable portraits of peasants: funny, eccentric and occasionally simple-minded, they also have wit, energy and vigour. In his notes to the play, he said that an actor playing a peasant should play an individual peasant, and that urban audiences will only understand the class as a whole when they see what connects the people that constitute that class. The crucial point is Brecht's enduring commitment to those at the bottom of society – wherever they come from.

Folk art is largely alien to modern western theatre – largely because the peasantry has disappeared in Europe and North America. But it has an important role to play in South American, Asian and African drama, where Brecht's insights into its enduring strengths are still seen as invaluable.

The 'New Objectivity'

The 'New Objectivity'[27] ('*Die Neue Sachlichkeit*') is the name given to a reaction in the 1920s against Expressionism, and a celebration, instead, of the straight lines of modernity. This international movement flowered in Weimar Germany, especially in the work of the Bauhaus, the Kroll Opera, the Festivals of New Music and John Heartfield's photo-collages. With the polarisation – and politicisation – of Weimar culture, it became increasingly identified with the left's response to Fascism; it also provided the aesthetic foundation for the entire post-war movement in design and architecture.

This desire for objectivity became increasingly important to Brecht, as he set out to encourage an attitude of critical distance towards what was being presented. But in thinking about it we must be careful. Above all, we must distinguish Brecht's aims from the Olympian objectivity of high classicism: Brecht isn't sitting above the fray, musing over the paradoxes of life. Instead, his insistence is inextricably allied to his commitment to a better world, and the one is meaningless without the other.

Such objectivity is fundamental to any art that tries to present a truthful – and contradictory – reflection of society. Although some of the external features of this are taken for granted today, the attempt to make drama scientifically objective is as valuable as ever. It is, perhaps, Brecht's most enduring legacy.

▶ See Exercises 19, 20, 21, 22 & 23 (Social Relationships)

The Land of the Free

One of the unforeseen consequences of the German defeat in the First World War was an unlikely romance with all things American. This was partly in reaction to Prussian militarism; it was also driven by a fascination with a culture that seemed dynamic and progressive. *Amerikanismus* permeated almost every aspect of the arts, and a fascination with 'the new world' is one of the defining characteristics of Weimar culture.

The Land of the Free offered Brecht an ideal location for his tales of struggle. Some of his best early plays are set in fantastical versions: *In the Jungle of the Cities*, *Saint Joan of the Stockyards* and *Arturo Ui* all take place in a mythical Chicago, while his only full-length opera, *Mahagonny*, unfolds in a Las

Vegas-type, Wild West free-for-all. When approaching these plays, we should remember America's contradictory appeal: its informality, energy and wide-open spaces, but also its iconic status as the home of dog-eat-dog capitalism. America offered Brecht an enticing alternative to provincial Germany while demonstrating both the splendours and the miseries of the very system he opposed.

Perhaps unsurprisingly, Brecht's love affair with America couldn't survive actually living there and, with the notable exception of *The Hollywood Elegies*, all his work written in California is set elsewhere. He wrote *The Chalk Circle* in America and was frank about the influence of the Broadway musical on its broad horizons: indeed, some would argue that it's almost sentimental as a result.

Amerikanismus has, of course, lost its lustre; after all, we're 'all Americans now'. But America is fundamental to Brecht's account of modern mores and his fascination should remind us of good drama's competitive, dynamic and confrontational spirit.

Cabaret and the Circus

Many of the giants of early twentieth-century culture saw the crude and anarchic as a way of breaking free of the decorative certainties of the nineteenth century. Pablo Picasso, James Joyce and Igor Stravinsky were all drawn to the cabaret and circus in their search for a unique kind of modern energy, and the Cabaret Voltaire in Zurich created Dadaism – a kind of punk art that celebrated the nonsensical, whose impact was felt right across Europe.

For all his later rationalism, the young Brecht was fascinated by such anarchy. He performed with the radical Bavarian clown Karl Valentin,[28] loved the political invectives of Karl Kraus and the satirical cabaret of Kurt Tucholsky, Walter Mehring and others. As a young director, he treated the theatre as a disposable art form, consisting of jokes, fragments and provocations, with little anxiety about how they are put together, and argued that only a popular, disposable theatre could say something meaningful about society.

Such theatricality is vividly on display in *Man Equals Man* and the accompanying one-act play *The Elephant Calf*. And one of Brecht's pre-war theatrical triumphs was his production of *The Baden-Baden Lesson on Consent*: when two clowns – discussing man's inhumanity to man – sawed off the wooden legs of a third, several members of the audience had to be carried out. Such raw energy lies at the heart of many of Brecht's most sophisticated theatrical ideas.

It's hard to recover the shock of such work, although the most satirical of modern comedians come close. The important point is the free and provocative relationship with the audience. Less pertinent is the modern circus (and some of the crasser products of 'physical theatre'), whose high-octane theatricality rarely communicates the world outside.

Expressionism

'Expressionism' dominated Northern Europe in the first years of the twentieth century. Its leading figures turned their backs on the scientific basis of naturalism and expressed their dreams and visions, fears and desires, with as much intensity as possible.

Expressionism was the leading progressive artistic form in Brecht's youth and he found it difficult to escape its influence. Indeed, it could be argued that Brecht's youthful theatre is nothing less than a working-out of his complex relationship with it. But his reaction was more than merely formal: he challenged its solipsistic self-indulgence and exalting of the mythological above the concrete, and the individual over the social:

> Expressionism vastly enriched the theatre's means of
> Expression and brought aesthetic gains that still have to
> be fully exploited, but it proved quite incapable of
> shedding light on the world as an object of human
> activity.[29]

This questioning of Expressionism's value lies at the heart of the evolution of Brecht's theatrical style.

In recent years, the modern British theatre has turned to Expressionism, often to impressive effect. But Brecht's objections are worth listening to: Expressionism replaces an analysis of society with the artist's private neuroses, and the modern Brechtian director and actor should question its underlying assumptions.

Modernism

'Modernism' was the other dominant cultural movement of Brecht's youth. Inspired by Rimbaud's dictum that 'one must be absolutely modern',[30] it insisted that all aspects of contemporary experience could – and should – be expressed in art.

Modernism's reaction against 'historicism' was largely a middle-class phenomenon and, at times, strikingly reactionary – even militaristic – in its tone.[31] So it's hardly surprising that Brecht's view was complex. He tended to dismiss its self-consciousness because of his desire to create socially useful drama; but, at the same time, he opposed narrow definitions of artistic form, and rejected the claim that only the 'realist' novel could provide a model for working–class art.[32]

With his particular combination of political commitment and radical form, Brecht occupies an uncomfortable niche in modernism's hall of fame. To understand, we need to recognise his commitment to contemporary forms, without forgetting his rejection of innovation for its own sake, free of political or social analysis. Balancing these two apparently contradictory positions provided Brecht with one of his richest dialectical resources.

For many reasons – above all, the collapse of the political causes that Brecht championed – a kind of apolitical and frequently modish modernism has triumphed in theatre. And when Brecht's work is praised, it's usually for its quality of modernism, not its political or social content. What's overlooked, perhaps, is Brecht's commitment to certain enduring values –

above all, peace and social justice. If we are to learn from
Brecht's example, we must see how he subjected even the most
contemporary of artistic form to these overarching imperatives.

The Russian Revolution and Radical Political Theatre

Brecht was not the first playwright to want the theatre to change
the world.

The Russian Revolution was committed to redressing social
inequalities and creating a different kind of man, and art was
expected to play its part. Meyerhold was the leading theatrical
figure but the movement included the Stanislavsky-influenced
theatre of Yevgeny Vakhtangov and the constructivism of
Alexander Tairov, as well as simple agitprop.

Although the spirit of the radical Soviet theatre was extin-
guished in the Stalinist assault on artistic experimentation, it was
enormously influential across Europe, especially at the Volksbühne in Berlin where Erwin Piscator directed a number of
groundbreaking theatrical events under its influence. The key feature of Piscator's work was the use of projectors, conveyor belts
and machinery to show human beings caught up in the imper-
sonality of the modern world. He turned his back on humanism
and tried to express contemporary life in all its violence:

> Piscator's experiments broke nearly all the conventions.
> They intervened to transform the playwright's creative
> methods, the actor's style of representation, and the work
> of the stage designer. They were striving towards an
> entirely new social function for the theatre.[33]

Piscator's influence on Brecht is most evident in *Man Equals
Man*, which shows how an ordinary man can be taken apart and
reassembled into 'a human fighting machine'; the fragmentary
Johann Fatzer, which tells of a soldier's return home from the
trenches of the First World War; and Brecht's gruesome epic
set in the Chicago meatpacking industry, *Saint Joan of the
Stockyards*.

Brecht admired Gorky enormously, and his dramatisation of *The Mother* stayed true to its social realism but, significantly, moved the action from 1905 to 1917, and employed the radical techniques and episodic structure of the *Lehrstücke*. The result was one of Brecht's greatest achievements.

Brecht's chief contribution to political theatre was a conscious rejection of this experimental modernity and the evolution, instead, of a classical style that placed human beings at the centre of everything:

> Here was a 'crisis: half a century's experiments, conducted in nearly every civilised country, had won the theatre a brand-new field of subject matter and types of problem, and made it a factor of marked social importance. At the same time they had brought the theatre to a point where any further development of the intellectual, social experience must wreck the artistic experience. And yet without further development of the former, the latter occurred less and less often. A technical apparatus and a style of acting had been evolved which could do more to stimulate illusions than to give experiences, more to intoxicate than to elevate, more to deceive than to illumine.[34]

Such apparently conservative questioning of experimentalism for its own sake should be as central to our understanding of Brecht's theatre as our celebration of his many innovations. Indeed, one valid criticism that can be levelled at Brecht is that by turning away from the experimental and the contemporary, Brecht's work – for all its materialism – became aesthetic and merely classical. It's a question that confronts the modern Brechtian today.

Existentialism

Perhaps the chief philosophical response to the disaster of the Second World War was existentialism. This held that all human effort was in vain and that the meaning of life lay in the bare facts of existence. It took artistic form in the works of Jean-Paul Sartre, Simone de Beauvoir, Eugène Ionesco, Samuel Beckett and others.[35]

Brecht regarded this movement with disdain, preferring a fuller engagement with the turmoils of society.[36] Nevertheless, his late poems betray a growing disillusionment with Soviet Communism and, occasionally, touch on the despair that was the basis for existential thinking. The last scene of *Mother Courage* presents an image of utter desolation and, among the papers found on Brecht's desk after his death was an edition of Beckett's *Waiting for Godot* with inconclusive pencil jottings in the margins. But critics who have drawn connections between Brecht's theatre and that of the absurdists have based their observations on superficial similarities. The two are philosophical opposites.

Conclusion

Brecht's theatre – and his theory – is exceptionally eclectic. He was inspired by art that was popular and rarefied, intellectual and instinctive, aesthetic and raw, emotional and austere. It's a common mistake to imagine that his taste was narrow or exclusive when, in fact, the opposite was the case.

But now it's time to see how Brecht brought all this together into a coherent whole. Like all the greatest twentieth-century artists, he achieved a unique fusion of the broadest range of influences.

1. The Communist historian Eric Hobsbawm used this phrase as the title for his autobiography, *Interesting Times: A Twentieth-Century Life* (2002).
2. 'To Those Born Later' (1938) is one of Brecht's greatest poems.
3. These include: John Willett, *Brecht in Context* (1984, revised 1994); Klaus Volker, *Brecht: A Biography* (1978); Ronald Hayman, *Brecht: A Biography* (1983); James K. Lyon, *Bertolt Brecht in America* (1982); Martin Esslin, *Brecht: A Choice of Evils* (1984); Ronald Speirs, *Bertolt Brecht* (1987); Eric Bentley, *The Brecht Memoir* (1991); Stephen Unwin, *A Guide to the Plays of Bertolt Brecht* (2005); and *The Cambridge Companion to Brecht* (2006).
4. See John Fuegi's *The Life and Lies of Bertolt Brecht* (1994); for a robust response see Michael Hofmann's review, reprinted in *Behind the Lines: Pieces on Writing and Pictures* (2002).
5. Three important exceptions are Willett's seminal *The Theatre of Bertolt Brecht: A Study from Eight Aspects* (1959); Fuegi's *Bertolt Brecht: Chaos According to Plan* (1987); and Meg Mumford's *Bertolt Brecht: Routledge Performance Practitioners* (2008).
6. See *Aesthetics and Politics* (1977), which assembles 'the key texts of the classic debate within German Marxism', by Theodor Adorno, Walter Benjamin, Ernst Bloch, Georg Lukács and Brecht himself.
7. See Erdmut Wizisla, *Walter Benjamin and Bertolt Brecht: the Story of a Friendship* (2009).
8. Cited in Willett, *The Theatre of Bertolt Brecht*.
9. Karl Marx, *Contribution to Critique of Hegel's Philosophy of Right* (1843).
10. For Exercise 9, rather than pitching plays, TV series or films, the actors could pitch stories from the Bible.
11. The most accessible translation of *The Poetics* is by Kenneth McLeish (NHB, 1999).
12. 'Short Description of a New Technique of Acting', Appendix (1940).
13. *Empedocles' Shoe* (2002) is the title of a volume of essays on Brecht's poetry.
14. Greek Theatre was predicated on the dialectical presentation of conflicting value systems, most powerfully through the *agon* where 'competing' characters give speeches that present opposing views. Brecht's *Antigone* demonstrates these dialectical contests particularly well.
15. 'The city must be a big, dusty uninhabitable place... some attention must be paid to countering the risk of chinoiserie. The vision is of a Chinese city's outskirts with cement works and so on. There are still gods around but aeroplanes have come in.'

16. See Edward Said *Orientalism* (1978).

17. *Journals 1934–1955.*

18. *The Prince of Homburg* was one of Hitler's favourite plays –
     presumably because the reluctant hero eventually submits to the
     power of the leader. My unrhyming translation of Brecht's Sonnet:

> O formal garden in the sands of Brandenburg!
> O dream vision in the Prussian blue night!
> O hero brought to his knees by the fear of death!
> O paragon of military pride and soldier's duty!
>
> Your backbone's cracked by the laurel wreath!
> You won the battle, but it wasn't yours to win.
> The Goddess of Victory doesn't smile on you here.
> Grinning, the Elector's executioner drags you off to the block.
>
> And so we see him, he who had rebelled,
> Washed and cleaned by the terror of death,
> His mortal sweat cold beneath the laurel leaf.
>
> His sword is still by his side: in pieces.
> He's not dead, but lying flat on his back:
> Down in the dust with all the enemies of Brandenburg!

19. Defending *The Mother* from the criticism that it was mere agitprop,
     Brecht claimed that 'features of the agitprop theatre were interwoven
     with legitimate forms of the classical German theatre (that of the
     youthful Schiller, Lenz, Goethe and Büchner)'.

20. Émile Zola, *Naturalism in the Theatre* (1881).

21. See 'Three Cheers for Shaw' (1926).

22. See, for example, the essay 'Some of the Things that can be learnt
     from Stanislavsky' (1952).

23. *Letters 1913–1956.*

24. Quoted in *Brecht in Context* (1998).

25. One of the most inspiring accounts of modern popular left-wing
     theatre is John McGrath's *A Good Night Out: Popular Theatre:
     Audience, Class and Form* (1981).

26. Brecht's essay, 'Notes on the Folk Play' (1940), draws some of these
     ideas together.

27. The best book on this movement is John Willett's *The New Sobriety*
     (1978).

28. Brecht contributed to a short film starring Valentin called *Mysteries
     of a Barbershop* (1923). He later credited Valentin with a crucial piece
     of theatrical advice: 'When the Augsburger [Brecht] was producing
     his first play, which included a thirty minutes' battle, he asked
     Valentin what he ought to do with the soldiers. "What are the

soldiers like in battle?" Valentin promptly answered: "They're pale. Scared shitless." '

29. 'On Experimental Theatre' (1939).

30. Arthur Rimbaud, 'Il faut être absolument moderne' from *A Season in Hell* (1873).

31. See Peter Gay's brilliant and sometimes shocking study *Modernism* (2009).

32. See *Aesthetics and Politics*.

33. 'On Experimental Theatre' (1939).

34. *Ibid.*

35. See Martin Esslin, *The Theatre of the Absurd* (1961). Esslin also wrote a book about Brecht entitled *A Choice of Evils* (1984), which shows a dramatist whose talent was betrayed by his political commitment.

36. See, for example, Brecht's satirical poem 'Encounter with the Poet Auden' in *Poems 1913–1956*.

2

In Theory

2

In Theory

WHY THEORY?

This book has been written for those many young actors, directors and writers who are drawn to Brecht's theatre and want to take up the 'Brecht challenge' into the twenty-first century. I'm aware that they may feel daunted by the extensive theory that confronts the student of Brecht, and my aim in this chapter is to clarify what he meant by the key terms. If I quote from the theory at length it's because I think we should read what Brecht actually wrote. In the rest of the book I will show how they can be taught and put into practice.

How to Approach It

But why is there so much theory and how should we approach it? First, we should recognise the intellectual nature of the German theatre. Even today German directors and playwrights are expected to describe their theoretical approach in detail, and the result is still highly conceptual. This contrasts with the commercial bias of the British theatre, which sets out, above all, to entertain, and where theories about writing, acting or the art of theatre are regarded with deep suspicion. There are many reasons for this – innate commercialism, the anti-intellectualism of British culture and a blithe assumption about the superiority of our theatre's way of working – but it can make Brecht's theory puzzling to the British reader.

And then, we need to take Brecht's theory with a bucketful of salt: apparently, when asked whether an English production of *Galileo* had created the 'alienation effect', Weigel replied that 'it was just a silly idea that Bert had come up with to stop his actors from overacting'. And there's nothing worse than doctrinaire 'Brechtian' productions which are mere exercises in theatrical style. In other words, we'd best approach Brecht's theoretical writings with some caution.

Above all, however, Brecht was an oppositional playwright, and shaped his theatre in reaction to what confronted him. He despised the mainstream theatre of his youth, and saw how many of its leading figures went on to support the Nazis. So it's hardly surprising that he felt the need to issue manifestos, essays and polemics. In exile, such activity was a surrogate for directing.

Finally, we should remember just how deliberately provocative so much of the theory is. Brecht wanted to encourage people to think about society in fresh and critical ways, and his theory speaks to its audience in the same dialectical and sly way that his plays do. Provocation requires overstatement, and Brecht often sets the volume too loud. But it's all part of his tactics.

Where to Find It

The British student is lucky that the theory is so readily available in carefully annotated and readable translations. The most important essays are *A Short Organum for the Theatre* and *The Messingkauf Dialogues*. Other key pieces can be found in *Brecht on Theatre*. There are notes by Brecht in the individual plays, some of which were written for the model books (see 'A Note on the Model Books', below) and the poems are rich with insights, as are the letters and journals. A recent volume of political essays[1] makes for fascinating reading, and the important debates on aesthetics between Brecht, Lukács, Adorno and Benjamin have been assembled in *Aesthetics and Politics*.[2]

Various people have expounded on Brecht's theory. Walter Benjamin's *Understanding Brecht* is a brilliant, if occasionally dense, collection of essays on the key ideas, including two attempts at answering the question 'What is Epic Theatre?' John Willett's definitive *Theatre of Bertolt Brecht* offers the most reliable account, and the same author's *Brecht in Context* explores the work in depth. Meg Mumford wrote a useful volume on the subject,[3] and my own guide to the plays includes introductory material to the theory.[4] And there are, of course, numerous academic studies.

Words and Definitions

One of the many difficulties faced by the student of Brecht's theory is the way that the various terms are so interlinked: thus it's impossible to describe the 'epic theatre' without reference to the 'alienation effect', or 'gestus' without 'contradiction' and 'complex seeing'. I've decided to define these terms individually, but they only make sense when read in conjunction with each other.

What's more, these headline terms are surrounded by dozens of other, less significant ones – many of which are only referred to occasionally – but all of which should be studied if we are to comprehend the scale of Brecht's achievements. And, as usual, it's essential to see all of this within its historical context. The crucial thing to remember is that everything in Brecht is informed by his underlying – and constantly evolving – response to the world around him. As ever, we have to read Brecht historically if we are to read him at all.

THE ALIENATION EFFECT

At the heart of Brecht's ambitions was the creation of a kind of theatre that would encourage audiences to think carefully about the society in which they lived, and decide to set about changing it. In 1940, he wrote:

> So the question is this: is it quite impossible to make the reproduction of real-life events the purpose of art and thereby make something conducive of the spectators' critical attitude toward them?

The 'alienation effect' – one of the most misunderstood terms in the Brechtian vocabulary – was the result.

Definitions

Strictly speaking, the German word *Verfremdung* should be translated as 'making strange' (*fremd* means strange): 'alienation' with its secondary sense of 'being alienated' – unpleasant, harsh and distant – has often led people to imagine that Brecht wanted a kind of theatre, and an acting style, that was cold or lacking in emotion. But 'alienation' (or 'A-effect', as it's sometimes called) is the usual translation, and we'd best stick to it.

The 'alienation effect' occurs when the audience is encouraged to question its preconceptions and look at the familiar in a new and different way – that is, to make it strange. In some respects, it's the artistic equivalent of the scientific method: just as the scientist examines natural phenomenon (an apple falling to the ground, the sun rising, heart attacks occurring) and questions traditional assumptions (the will of the apple, the movement of the sun, God's punishment for bad deeds), so the theatre presents an event (the crowning of a king, the power of a landowner, the rise of Fascism) and helps the audience challenge received opinions about what is being shown. In the same way that science proceeds from evidence, so art – Brecht argued – should take nothing for granted. The 'alienation effect' was essential for such questioning.

The 'alienation effect' wasn't new: Brecht took it from a huge range of sources – 'the Chinese theatre, the Spanish classical theatre, the popular theatre of Breughel's day and the Elizabethan theatre'.[5] The key difference is the purpose for which it's being used:

> The old A-effects quite remove the object represented from the spectator's grasp, turning it into something that cannot be altered; the new are not odd in themselves, though the unscientific eye stamps anything strange as odd. The new alienations are only designed to free

socially conditioned phenomena from that stamp of familiarity which protects them against our grasp today.[6]

In other words, Brecht's achievement was to adapt the 'alienation effect' into a style appropriate for the modern world.

In Practice

To induce the 'alienation effect', everyone involved in staging a production needs to know what the writer thinks about the events portrayed, and let this understanding affect every aspect of his work. This requires a level of intellectual, moral and political involvement that most modern approaches to the theatre ignore. The important point is that Brecht knew that there are many different degrees of intellectual understanding, and that the 'alienation effect' is only valuable if the analysis is sophisticated.

Thus, in staging *Fear and Misery*, Brecht's great cycle of one-act plays about life in the pre-war Third Reich, the actors aren't asked just to remind us that Fascism is bad; instead, he expects them to demonstrate – with forensic insight – the attraction that Fascism holds for certain people in particular situations. Unlike the modern (and frankly sentimental) emphasis on 'positive role models', or drama 'from the perspective of the victims', Brecht wanted to provoke his audience into working out why people so often do things which are not in their best interest.

Producing the 'alienation effect' requires a kind of double vision from the actor, who needs both to inhabit his character and remember that he is showing it. The danger with identification, Brecht argued, is that it prevents the actor from commenting on what is happening and thus stops the performance from having an active effect. Instead, he wanted 'the actor to discard whatever means he has learnt of getting the audience to identify itself with the characters which he plays':

Aiming not to put his audience into a trance, he must not go into a trance himself. His muscles must remain loose, for a turn of the head, e.g. with tautened neck muscles,

will 'magically' lead the spectators' eyes and even their
heads to turn with it, and this can only detract from any
speculation or reaction which the gesture may bring
about. His way of speaking has to be free from parsonical
sing-song and from all those cadences which lull the
spectator so that the sense gets lost. Even if he plays a
man possessed he must not seem to be possessed himself,
for how is the spectator to discover what possessed him if
he does?[7]

This emphasis on relaxation and ease is fundamental, and an
important corrective to the assumption that the 'alienation
effect' is difficult to achieve.

Emotion has an important role to play, but in a different way:

At no moment must [the actor] go so far as to be wholly
transformed into the character played. The verdict: 'he
didn't act Lear, he was Lear' would be an annihilating
blow to him. He has just to show the character, or rather
he has to do more than just get into it; this does not mean
that if he is playing passionate parts he must remain cold.
It is only that his feelings must not at bottom be those of
the character, so that the audience's may not at bottom be
those of the character either. The audience must have
complete freedom here.[8]

The essay on Chinese acting elaborates on this sense of distance
between actor and part, and offers perhaps his clearest definition of the practical implementations:

The alienation effect does not in any way demand an
unnatural way of acting. It has nothing whatever to do
with ordinary stylisation. On the contrary, the
achievement of the A-effect absolutely depends on
lightness and naturalness of performance. But when the
actor checks the truth of his performance... he is not just
thrown back on his 'natural sensibilities', but can always
be corrected by a comparison with reality... And so from

outside, by other people, he acts in such a way that nearly every sentence could be followed by a verdict of the audience and practically every gesture is submitted for the public's approval.[9]

This rejection of an 'unnatural way of acting' and insistence on a direct 'comparison with reality' is an important corrective to the common misapprehension that the 'alienation effect' is in some sense artificial.

But Brecht went further. Talking about a production which successfully induced the 'alienation effect', he noted:

The spectator was no longer in any way allowed to submit to an experience uncritically (and without practical consequences) by means of simple empathy with the characters in a play. The production took the subject matter and the incidents shown and put them through a process of alienation that is necessary to all understanding. When something seems 'the most obvious thing in the world' it means that any attempt to understand the world has been given up.[10]

Whereas traditional theatre (and self-indulgent acting) strives merely for empathy, Brecht's theatre attempted something much more dynamic:

Conventional actors devote their efforts so exclusively to bringing about this psychological operation [empathy] that they may be said to see it as the principal aim of their art... the technique which produces an A-effect is the exact opposite of that which aims at empathy.[11]

He quickly qualified this, however, recognising that 'empathy' cannot be entirely avoided and, once again, drew on everyday experience to provide the actor with his criteria:

Yet in his efforts to reproduce particular characters and show their behaviour [the actor] need not renounce the means of empathy entirely. He uses these means just as

any normal person with no particular acting talent would
use them if he wanted to portray someone else... This
showing of other people's behaviour happens time and
again in ordinary life... without those involved making
the least effort to subject their spectators to an illusion.[12]

As usual in Brecht, the qualifications are as important as the
main argument.

The crucial point is that Brecht wanted his actors to tell their
characters' story with as much objectivity as possible: like someone who has seen a car crash or a spectator at a football match
might describe it, drawing attention to the decisive moments,
asking the listeners to look at what happened from a variety of
perspectives, and helping them come to their own judgement, so
actors should approach their performance with a keen eye, above
all, on 'what needs to be shown', and edit everything else away.

An actor playing Macbeth shouldn't simply aim for the audience's sympathy at the great man's downfall, he should show the
steps that took him to power, and the murderous deeds – and
many victims – that defined his tyranny. Similarly, someone
playing Lear should avoid the conclusion that the king is the
victim of his daughters' 'evil' and accept, instead, that he is
using arbitrary powers in an irrational and foolish way and that
his madness has a direct correlative in the disorder of his country. Similarly, an actress playing Mother Courage should show
that the death of her children is the direct result of her own
actions and that, at heart, she is a moderately successful small
businesswoman, trying to make a living off the war, just as an
actor playing Galileo should demonstrate that scientific advance
isn't morally or socially neutral: thrilling as 'pure science' can
seem, it can be used for ill as easily as good, and the modern
philosopher would accept that complex truth.

What's more, the actor should retain throughout an awareness of the artificiality of what is happening:

Just as the actor no longer has to persuade the audience
that it is the author's character and not himself that is

standing on stage, so also he need not pretend that the events taking place on the stage have never been rehearsed, and are now happening for the first and only time… It should be apparent all through his performance that 'even at the start and in the middle he knows how it ends' and he must 'thus maintain a calm independence throughout'.[13]

All of this will encourage the audience to look at what is being presented with greater degrees of scepticism and critical objectivity.

We need to be very careful when talking about the 'alienation effect'. Not only did Brecht's own actors perform with tremendous emotional fluency, but many modern actors and directors with sympathy for Brecht's overall objectives regard the 'alienation effect' as little more than carefully observed realism, presented in a fragmentary form. The 'alienation effect' doesn't need a particularly strange kind of acting: it just needs attention to the details of the play and a refusal to overwhelm the audience with demands for individual empathy. Everything should be performed with passion and power, but also with clarity and wit, and as great a degree of objectivity as possible. *The Messingkauf Dialogues* offers the most concise statement of all:

> To achieve the A–effect the actor must give up his *complete conversion* into the stage character. He *shows* the character, he *quotes* his lines, he *repeats* a real-life incident. The audience is not entirely 'carried away'…[14]

Brecht in Rehearsal

Brecht wanted to promote a kind of acting that has quotation marks around it: 'this is what happened', 'this is who got hurt', 'this is who won the battle', and so on. He expected his actors to tell the story in such a way that the individual elements can be seen as temporary and subject to change – a long way from a theatre that offers its audience unshakeable 'eternal truths'. The effect is twofold: it helps the actor present each moment with great clarity, and it allows him to demonstrate his own attitude to what is being shown.

Brecht sometimes asked his actors in rehearsal to perform in the third person, prefacing each speech with 'he said... she said...' At other times, he made them highlight particularly important moments by adding 'instead of responding like this, he responded like that'. At other times he asked them to read the stage directions aloud. And he would talk constantly, soliciting opinions from his assistant directors, passing technicians, observers, and the actors themselves. He wanted his actors to do two things at once: play the scene and provoke a discussion with the audience about its content.

Acting in such a way that produces the 'alienation effect' means nothing less than subordinating everything to the communication of simple and useful insights into the workings of the world outside.

On Stage

Producing the 'alienation effect' in the audience requires more than just a particular approach to acting. It affects all aspects of the physical production:

> The stage and auditorium must be purged of everything 'magical' and no 'hypnotic tensions' should be set up. This ruled out any attempt to make the stage convey the flavour of a particular place... or to create atmosphere by relaxing the tempo of the conversation. The audience was not 'worked up' by a display of temperament or 'swept away' by acting with tautened muscles; in short, no attempt was made to put it into a trance and give it the illusion of watching an ordinary unrehearsed event.[15]

Brecht emphasised the importance of maintaining a continuous awareness of the audience (fundamental to Shakespearean acting) and the value of direct address:

It is of course necessary to drop the assumption that there is a fourth wall cutting the audience off from the stage and the consequent illusion that the stage action is taking place in reality and without an audience. That being so, it is possible for the actor in principle to address the audience direct.[16]

And, of course, the 'alienation effect' has an impact on every aspect of the design and lighting, as I will show later.

▶ See Exercises 30, 31, 32, 33 & 34 (Alienation) and 35, 36, 37, 38 & 39 (Moments of Decision)

EPIC THEATRE

Brecht's theatre deliberately avoids the sense of tragic inevitability that is such a feature of classical drama. 'Fate', the Marxist argues, implies that we have no powers of self-determination and robs us of the opportunity to change our situation for the better. In response to this, and inspired by Shakespeare above all, Brecht came up with the notion of the 'epic theatre', which he declared 'appeals less to the feelings than to the spectator's reason'.[17]

Definitions

It's sometimes thought that 'epic theatre' refers only to large-scale historical dramas. Of course, as a Marxist, Brecht cared about history, and his plays often described a large sweep of time and referred to actual historical events. But the term is best used to describe a technique more than a genre: *The Mother* and *Fear and Misery of the Third Reich* are as much 'epic theatre' as *Mother Courage*, *Galileo* or *The Caucasian Chalk Circle*.

Brecht tried to define 'epic theatre' on many occasions. There are no absolute statements, but perhaps the clearest is this:

The epic theatre is chiefly interested in the attitudes
which people adopt towards one another, wherever they
are socio-historically significant. It works out scenes
where people adopt attitudes of such a sort that the social
laws under which they are acting spring into sight… The
concern of the epic theatre is thus eminently practical.
Human behaviour is shown as alterable; man himself as
dependent on certain political and economic factors and
at the same time as capable of altering them.[18]

The epic is evident wherever art deliberately pastes together
conflicting elements, be it classical theatre, popular culture,
photomontage or Dadaism, and Brecht was frank about its
various roots:

Stylistically speaking, there is nothing at all that is new
about the epic theatre. Its expository character and its
emphasis in virtuosity bring it close to the old Asiatic
theatre. Didactic tendencies are to be found in the medieval
mystery and the classical Spanish theatre, and also in the
theatre of the Jesuits. These theatrical forms corresponded
to particular trends of their time, and vanished with them.[19]

His great achievement was to borrow from all these sources and
develop a radical theatrical technique of his own.

Walter Benjamin offers one of the most useful definitions of
the 'epic theatre':

Epic theatre, by contrast [to Aristotelian theatre],
advances by fits and starts, like the images on a film strip.
Its basic form is that of the forceful impact on one
another of separate, distinct situations in the play. The
songs, the captions included in the stage décor, the
gestural conventions of the actors, serve to separate each
situation. Thus distances are created everywhere which
are, on the whole, detrimental to illusion among the
audience. These distances are meant to make the
audience adopt a critical attitude, to make it think.[20]

Brecht was similarly keen to chart the difference between the 'epic theatre' and the conventional 'dramatic theatre',[21] and came up with a striking formulation:

> The dramatic theatre's spectator says: Yes, I have felt like that too – Just like me – It's only natural – It'll never change – The sufferings of this man appal me, because they are inescapable – That's great art; it all seems the most obvious thing in the world – I weep when they weep, I laugh when they laugh.

> The epic theatre's spectator says: I'd never have thought it – That's not the way – That's extraordinary, hardly believable – It's got to stop – The sufferings of this man appal me, because they are unnecessary – That's great art: nothing obvious in it – I laugh when they weep, I weep when they laugh.[22]

Brecht's essay 'The Modern Theatre is the Epic Theatre' has a large table which shows these differences vividly.

Brecht was eager to scotch the notion that the 'epic theatre' is in some sense unemotional, and said that:

> The essential point is that it appeals less to the feelings than to the spectator's reason. Instead of sharing an experience the spectator must come to grips with things. At the same time it would be quite wrong to try and deny emotion to this kind of theatre. It would be much the same thing as trying to deny emotion to modern science.[23]

As ever, Brecht took much of his inspiration from the everyday, and described a street scene in which two men offer different accounts about what happened in a traffic accident. He goes out of his way to explain its relevance for the kind of 'major theatre' he was trying to create:

> Such an example of the most primitive type of epic theatre seems easy to understand. Yet experience has

shown that it presents astounding difficulties to the
reader or listener as soon as he is asked to see the
implications of treating this kind of street-corner
demonstration as a basic form of major theatre, theatre
for a scientific age. What this means of course is that the
epic theatre may appear richer, more intricate and
complex in every particular, yet to be major theatre it
need at bottom only contain the same elements as a
street-corner demonstration of this sort; nor could it any
longer be termed epic theatre if any of the main elements
of the street-corner demonstration were lacking. Until
one understands the novelty, unfamiliarity and direct
challenge to the critical faculties of the suggestion that
street-corner demonstrations of this sort can serve as a
satisfactory basis model of major theatre, one cannot
really understand what follows.[24]

Walter Benjamin answers the somewhat technical question
'What is Epic Theatre?' with startling effect:[25]

Epic theatre takes account of a circumstance which has
received too little attention, and which could be
described as the filling-in of the orchestra pit. The abyss
which separates the actors from the audience like the
dead from the living, the abyss whose silence heightens
the sublime in drama and whose resonance heightens the
intoxication of opera – the abyss which, of all the
elements of the stage, bears most indelibly the traces of
its sacral origins, has increasingly lost its significance.
The stage is still elevated. But it no longer rises from an
immeasurable depth: it has become a public platform.
The didactic play and epic theatre set out to occupy this
platform.

Brecht's 'epic theatre', Benjamin argues, fundamentally changes
the role of drama in society.

A New Form for the New Realities

Throughout his life, Brecht maintained that the bewildering disjointedness of modern life required a new approach in art. Defending his innovations against the charge that they were 'formalist', Brecht was clear that he was simply developing a theatrical form suitable for the new realities:

> The first thing therefore is to comprehend the new subject matter; the second to shape the new relations. The reason: art follows reality. An example: the extraction and refinement of petroleum spirit represents a new complex of subjects, and when one studies these carefully one becomes struck by quite new forms of human relationship. A particular mode of behaviour can be observed both in the individual and in the mass, and it is clearly peculiar to the petroleum complex. But it wasn't the new mode of behaviour that created this particular way of refining petrol. The petroleum complex came first, and the new relationships are secondary... Petroleum resists the five-act form; today's catastrophes do not progress in a straight line but in cyclical crises; the 'heroes' change with the different phases, etc.... It is impossible to explain a present-day character by features or a present-day action by motives that would have been adequate in our fathers' time.[26]

The crucial point is that, for Brecht, formal innovations are a direct result of the new realities and not the other way round. Hence my insistence throughout on an understanding of the social and political context in which Brecht was working which is, of course, crucial if we are to understand the 'epic theatre'.

To summarise then: in the 'epic theatre', stories are told through a collage of contrasting scenes, whose content, style and approach are deliberately incongruous. Interruptions are encouraged, text is set against action, music is introduced, scenery is cut away, unconnected scenes follow on from each other, and a new kind of artistic unity emerges. By exposing the audience to such a broad range of conflicting elements, Brecht hoped they would think independently and come to their own conclusions. And so, the 'epic theatre' is nothing less than dialectics in practice.

In Practice

Actors and directors in the 'epic theatre' should see the play as a collection of incidents that demonstrate different aspects of character according to changing circumstances. They should relish the contradictions that this technique reveals and not attempt to smooth out the differences. They should be careful to 'play one thing after another' and not impose consistency or smoothness: they should, instead, embrace the jagged, disconnected elements of the story.

An example might be Yvette, the prostitute in *Mother Courage*. When we first meet her, business is bad because all her customers know that she is riddled with venereal disease; but the arrival of the Catholic army changes her situation dramatically (new clients who don't know her). It's when she has become a rich woman that the transformation is the most extreme: the audience knows that she is still Yvette, but the actress needs to show just how different she is – wealthy, fat and powerful. Similarly, an 'epic theatre' production would emphasise the contrasting phases of Macbeth's descent into violent tyranny (and not regard him as a murderous monster from the outset), as well as chart the emergence of the opposition. Change is what matters in the 'epic theatre', not stasis.

Brecht was aware of the way that this might be perceived:

> The epic actor's efforts to make particular incidents
> between human beings seem striking... may also cause
> him to be misrepresented as a short-range episodist by
> anybody who fails to allow for his way of knotting all the
> separate incidents together and absorbing them in the
> broad flow of his performance. As against the dramatic
> actor, who has his character established from the first and

simply exposes it to the inclemencies of the world and the tragedy, the epic actor lets his character grow before the spectator's eyes out of the way in which he behaves. 'This way of joining up', 'this way of selling an elephant', 'this way of conducting the case', do not altogether add up to a single unchangeable character but to one which changes all the time and becomes more and more clearly defined in the course of 'this way of changing'.[27]

But this very quality of change and contradiction is central to Brecht's purposes.

The 'epic theatre' is the theatrical form in which the 'alienation effect' is most appropriate, and shares many of the same characteristics. And so Brecht asked his actors to be involved in the practical presentation of the play – resetting props and scenery, putting on new costumes, etc. – all in full view. The aim of this was to remind audiences that what they're seeing is provisional, a gesture towards illusion, but above all a presentation of a world that is capable of being changed. The bright lights, the white cyclorama, the clear staging, the remorseless focus on reality and how it can be changed: the manifold features of the 'epic theatre' have the simplest and most direct of intentions:

> The epic theatre uses the simplest possible groupings, such as express the event's overall sense. No more 'casual', 'lifelike', 'unforced' grouping; the stage no longer reflects the 'natural' disorder of things. The opposite of natural disorder is aimed at: natural order. This order is determined from a social-historical point of view.[28]

Brecht wanted to encourage his audience to think critically about what was being presented, and to see 'natural' events – the rise of Hitler is the best example – as unnatural and resistible. The 'epic theatre' – allied to the 'alienation effect' – is the best way of achieving that.

▶ See Exercises 1, 2 ,3 ,4, 5 & 6 (The Ensemble) and 7, 8, 9, 10, 11 & 12 (Story and Narrative)

GESTUS

Brecht wanted to create a kind of theatre that made its points with all the vivid clarity of a biblical parable. He was more interested in the relationships between people than in their individual experiences, and saw character as the result of social conditions and not the other way round. Furthermore, his aesthetic was highly figurative and he admired the presence of the human figure in Christian, oriental and classical art. He was fascinated by the realism of such work and the three-dimensionality of the best of it.

Brecht borrowed the term 'gestus' from Lessing's *Hamburger Dramaturgie* (1767) and used it as a way of describing the physical expression of relationships between people in society. It's one of the most important concepts in the Brechtian theatre.

Definitions

At its simplest, 'gestus' is like the English word 'gesture': the pointed finger, the shrugged shoulder, the turned back, and so on. Brecht was keen that his stage pictures should express as powerfully as possible what was happening in the story and hoped his audience could grasp the key relationships by looking at a single moment of action. He insisted that every moment of his productions at the Berliner Ensemble should be photographed, and the results demonstrate vividly the power of the 'gestus' in action.

'Gestus' (or 'gest') refers to something deeper, however: an embodiment of the social relationships. Brecht came up with his own definition:

> 'Gest' is not supposed to mean gesticulation: it is not a
> matter of explanatory or emphatic movements of the
> hands, but of overall attitudes. A language is 'gestic' when
> it is grounded in a gest and conveys particular attitudes
> adopted by the speaker towards other men. The sentence

'pluck the eye that offends thee out' is less effective from
the gestic point of view than 'if thine eye offend thee,
pluck it out'. The latter starts by presenting the eye, and
the first clause has the definite gest of making an
assumption; the main clause then comes as a surprise, a
piece of advice, and a relief.[29]

Brecht was aware that it's possible to use 'gests' in different ways
and stresses their social content above all:

Not all gests are social gests. The attitude of chasing away
a fly is not yet a social gest, though the attitude of chasing
away a dog may be one, for instance if it comes to
represent a badly dressed man's continual battle against
watchdogs... The gest of working is definitely a social
gest, because all human activity directed towards the
mastery of nature is a social undertaking, an undertaking
between men. On the other hand a gest of pain, as long
as it is kept so abstract and generalised that it does not
rise above a purely animal category, is not yet a social one.
But this is precisely the common tendency of art: to
remove the social element in any gest. The artist is not
happy till he achieves 'the look of a hunted animal'. The
man then becomes just Man; his gest is stripped of any
social individuality; it is an empty one, not representing
any undertaking or operation among men by this
particular man. The 'look of a hunted animal' can
become a social gest if it is shown that particular
manoeuvres by men can degrade the individual man to
the level of a beast; the social gest is the gest relevant to
society, the gest that allows conclusions to be drawn
about the social circumstances.[30]

Each 'gestus' captures a particular set of interlocking attitudes,
and the sum total offers the audience a chart of the society that
is portrayed, and provides a physical expression of a range of
particular social and political analyses:

The realm of attitudes adopted by the characters towards
one another is what we call the realm of gest. Physical
attitude, tone of voice and facial expression are all
determined by a social gest: the characters are cursing,
flattering, instructing one another, and so on. The
attitudes which people adopt towards one another
include even those attitudes which would appear to be
quite private, such as the utterances of physical pain in an
illness, or of religious faith. These expressions of a gest
are usually highly complicated and contradictory, so that
they cannot be rendered by any single word and the actor
must take care that in giving his image the necessary
emphasis he does not lose anything, but emphasises the
entire complex.[31]

Thus 'gestus' presents human relationships as shaped by their
underlying social circumstances and – especially when presented
as 'epic theatre' and inducing the 'alienation effect' – holds them
up to scrutiny in such a way that they seem changeable.

In Practice

In essence, 'gestus' means presenting action with quotation
marks around it (a direct extension of the 'alienation effect'):
'this is how a woman stands who is pretending not to recognise
the body of her son so that she can maintain her business'; 'this
is how a scientist sits who is pretending that he has given up on
the pursuit of scientific truth'; 'this is how a judge passes judg-
ment who, by having no understanding of the law, is most likely
to give the poor justice', and so on.

Understanding the 'gestus' of each individual moment is
essential. Thus the way that Galileo teaches Andrea about the
orbit of the earth around the sun has a different 'gestus' from
the way he pretends that the telescope he gives to the Doge is
his own invention: the contrast between the two goes to the
heart of the meaning of the play. Similarly, the way that Mother
Courage, all alone at the end, hauls the cart around the stage

for the last time, still looking for business, is a unique and troubling 'gestus': Brecht's great 1949 production showed a desperate woman determined to continue living off the very war that had robbed her of everything – children, love and material well-being.

Brecht saw 'gests' everywhere and they became the building blocks of his productions:

> Each single incident has its basic gest: *Richard Gloucester courts his victim's widow. The child's true mother is found by means of a chalk circle. God has a bet with the Devil for Dr Faustus's soul. Woyzeck buys a cheap knife in order to do his wife in,* etc. The grouping of the characters on the stage and the movements of the groups must be such that the necessary beauty is attained above all by the elegance with which the material conveys that the gest is set out and laid bare to the understanding of the audience.[32]

Brecht was keen to emphasise that a performance should be made up of a series of such 'gests', many of which might seem strikingly contradictory (see 'Contradiction and Complex Seeing', below). Having described a sequence of 'gests' in the first scene of *Galileo*, he addresses the actor directly:

> Splitting such material into one gest after another, the actor masters his character by first mastering the 'story'. It is only after walking all round the entire episode that he can, as it were by a single leap, seize and fix his character, complete with all its individual features. Once he has done his best to let himself be amazed by the inconsistencies in its various attitudes, knowing that he will in turn have to make them amaze the audience, then the story as a whole gives him a chance to pull the inconsistencies together.[33]

Thus, acting with 'gestus' requires an understanding of the entire play and a desire to share that understanding with the audience.

To help with this, Brecht would sometimes ask his actors to preface each action with a little comment: 'this is how the land-lord pays his peasants wages', 'let me show you how the able-bodied beggar takes on the pose of a wounded war hero', 'look how Mother Courage defends her stock from demands for charity', and so on. The point was to encourage a kind of acting that was playful and objective and demonstrated individual observations with a set of clearly defined physical attitudes, which could be easily understood. This even extended to the way that the actors should offer the play up to the audience:

> One more thing: the delivery to the audience of what has
> been built up in the rehearsals. Here it is essential that
> the actual playing should be infused with the gest of
> handing over a finished article. What now comes before
> the spectator is the most frequently repeated of what has
> not been rejected, and so the finished representations
> have to be delivered with the eyes fully open, so that they
> may be received with the eyes open too.[34]

Walter Benjamin said that 'Epic theatre is gestural', and 'gestic theatre' is nothing less than a dramatic and physical demon-stration of the way that the world works. It's quite a claim.

▶ See Exercises 24, 25, 26, 27, 28 & 29 (Gestus), 3, 4 & 5 (The Ensemble) and 48 (Contemporary Images)

CONTRADICTION AND COMPLEX SEEING

At the heart of classical tragedy is the fatal flaw, the 'contradiction' that brings about the catastrophe. The greatest plays offer us a Hegelian syllogism, a conflict of opposites: one group wants one thing, another wants the opposite and the disagreement between the two resolves itself into a third position. This is fundamental to the patterning of Greek tragedy, the dynamic clashes of Shakespeare and the settled power of neoclassical drama. And it's also evident in the three-dimensional characterisation of the best nineteenth-century drama. In Brecht, however, contradiction became the defining characteristic of the dramatic method and is fundamental to his theatrical style.

Story of an Obsession

Brecht was obsessed by 'contradiction' in all its forms, and one of his great innovations was to make this the central subject of his writing. He increasingly argued that identifying such contradictions wasn't just important for verisimilitude, but was a precondition for resolving them. He declared that 'Contradictions are our hope!'[35] and their deliberate use is everywhere you look in his theatre.

In the early plays this obsession can be found in the constant clash of stylistic registers: the sentimental followed by the cynical, the intellectual by the sensual, the rational by the sensual. The result is that every argument appears in relative terms and emotions are, for the most part, satirised and undermined. If the result was largely negative, it cleared the way for Brecht's more mature understanding of the way that contradictions inherent in society appear in the make-up of the individual.

In his late work, this interest became more positive. His reading of Voltaire and the other *philosophes* of the Enlightenment, as well as classical Chinese philosophy, turned it into an exercise in dialectical thinking: 'on the one hand this, on the other hand that' was, he felt, the approach that stood most chance of approximating to the truth of the world.[36]

Complex Seeing

As his political understanding developed, Brecht became more and more interested in what he called 'complex seeing'. This is something much more dynamic than stoical despair at the contradictions of the world; instead, Brecht asked his actors to make these contradictions visible, and show the link between wealth and poverty, money and power, injustice and greed. By exposing the different sides of the argument, he hoped to encourage understanding and provoke debate.

Thus, in writing *The Caucasian Chalk Circle*, Brecht was keen to show that his 'heroine', Grusha, was a 'sucker' (he used the American term) in following her 'natural' maternal instincts, and argued that she would have been better off if she had ignored the abandoned aristocratic baby, Michael, and devoted her energies to looking after herself. Similarly, he maintained that Adzak isn't a clever peasant judge with sympathies for his own class, but is, instead, deeply corrupt; Brecht's shocking conclusion is that it's only in conditions of such corruption that the poor stand any chance of obtaining justice – and that in a badly run world, such 'maternal instincts' are self-destructive.

The point is that these observations are deliberately counter-intuitive and make us rethink our usual notions of 'common sense' or 'nature'. The techniques of the 'epic theatre', the 'alienation effect' and 'gestus' all bring out the contradictions inherent in the work, and in the world: complex seeing is fundamental.

In Practice

Many of Brecht's greatest characters are designed on deliberately contradictory principles: thus, the 'good woman', Shen Teh, becomes a bad man, Shui Ta, in order to survive; Mother Courage sacrifices her children so as to make a living; Galileo abandons pure scientific pursuit because of its personal implications; and Puntila, who is generous when drunk, reverts to brutality when sober. The point is that these contradictions are not the result of bad writing – they are deliberate and realistic portraits of the way that people behave in a contradictory world.

Contradictions, Brecht believed, express underlying realities:

> The bourgeois theatre's performances always aim at
> smoothing over contradictions, at creating false harmony,
> at idealisation. Conditions are reported as if they could
> not be otherwise; characters as individuals, incapable by
> definition of being divided, cast in one block, manifesting

themselves in the most various situations, likewise for that matter existing without any situation at all. If there is any development it is always steady, never by jerks; the developments always take place within a definite framework which cannot be broken through. None of this is like reality, so a realistic theatre must give it up.[37]

When working in a Brechtian fashion we should do everything we can to show up these deliberate and carefully constructed contradictions, wherever they occur.

▶ See Exercises 40, 41, 42, 43, 44 & 45 (Contradiction/ Complex Seeing) and 35, 36, 37, 38 & 39 (Moments of Decision)

OTHER KEY TERMS

Brecht's theoretical writings throw up a vast range of other concepts, most of which are related to – and support – the terms already discussed. For the most part less technical, they nevertheless cast important light on the scale of Brecht's ambitions for the theatre.

Realism

Brecht frequently argued that his theatrical innovations were simply a way of bringing a greater degree of 'realism' to his portrayals of modern experience. Just as the Cubists claimed that their paintings – by combining a variety of perspectives – were a truer portrayal of their subjects than Impressionism, so Brecht insisted that his theatrical style was a better way of depicting the reality of twentieth-century life than the techniques offered by nineteenth-century naturalism. The word Brecht insisted on was 'realism'.

'Realism' is notoriously difficult to define. It's best regarded as an attitude to the world, not an artistic style in its own right. Brecht's own definition is typically provocative:

> The usual view is that the more easily reality can be
> recognised in a work of art, the more realistic it is.
> Against this I would like to set up the equation that the
> more recognisably reality is mastered in the work of art,
> the more realistic it is.[38]

Behind this apparent sleight of hand, Brecht's notion of 'realism' is actually quite straightforward. Above all, it asks difficult questions about the material basis of life ('Who built the Great Wall of China?' asks one of Brecht's best poems) and is highly sceptical of those in power. It rejects shallow moralising and understands that survival is the most important thing for the poor and wretched: 'Food first, morals later,' as *The Threepenny Opera* warns.

Furthermore, Brecht's 'realistic' attitude to the world is morally relative and recognises that the 'ends' sometimes justify the 'means'. It also realises that history is made up of conflict and contradiction, and that the future is up for grabs. Most controversially, it insists on telling stories from the perspective of 'the revolutionary working class':

> The words Popularity and Realism therefore are natural
> companions. It is in the interest of the people, the broad
> working masses, that literature should give them truthful
> representations of life; and truthful representations of
> life are in fact only of use to the broad working masses,
> the people; so that they have to be suggestive and
> intelligible to them, i.e. popular...[39]

Brecht knew that there were many different ways of being 'realistic' and that 'realism' did not require the narrow constraints of 'naturalism':

> Anybody who is not bound by formal prejudices knows
> that there are many ways of suppressing truth and many
> ways of stating it: that indignation at inhuman conditions
> can be stimulated in many ways, by direct descriptions of
> a pathetic or matter-of-fact kind, by narrating stories and

parables, by jokes, by over- and understatement. In the theatre, reality can be represented in a factual or fantastic form. The actors can do without make-up, appearing 'natural', and the whole thing can be a fake; they can wear grotesque masks and represent the truth. There is not much to argue about here: the means must be asked what the end is.[40]

In the 1930s, Brecht found himself in a fascinating argument about left-wing aesthetics, and the issues raised are still relevant. In essence, the Marxist critic Georg Lukács argued for the enduring value of the 'realist' tradition, as evident in the great nineteenth-century novelists (Dickens, Balzac and Tolstoy), and accused Brecht of turning his back on the working class. The charge was of artistic formalism, and Brecht was accused of being a decadent writer more interested in artistic innovation than in reaching out to popular audiences.

This led to a lively (frequently bad-tempered) discussion.[41] Brecht – supported by Walter Benjamin – defended the enduring value of radical forms. He argued that working people had the least to lose in abandoning the old ways and were uniquely suited to enjoy radical and progressive art. More importantly, he turned the charge of 'formalism' against his accusers, and stated that his innovations were dictated by the new content and not the other way round. Those who insisted on traditional forms were, he argued, the real 'formalists':

> We must not abstract the one and only realism from certain given works, but shall make a lively use of all means, old and new, tried and untried, deriving from art and deriving from other sources, in order to put living reality in the hands of living people in such a way that it can be mastered. We shall take care not to ascribe realism to a particular historical form of novel belonging to a particular period, Balzac's or Tolstoy's, for instance, so to set up merely formal and literary criteria of realism. We shall not restrict ourselves to speaking of realism in cases

where one can smell, look, feel whatever is being
depicted, where 'atmosphere' is created and stories
develop in such a way that the characters are
psychologically stripped down. Our conception of
realism needs to be broad and political, free from
independent restrictions and independent of
convention.[42]

It's a powerful argument and Lukács's position was nothing less
than orthodox Marxism's critique of modernism. And Brecht's
position feels more amenable to the modern, liberal sensibility.

As time goes by, this debate looks ever more complex. First,
it's unfair to dismiss Lukács as a Communist apparatchik,
devoted to Socialist Realism; in fact, the popularity across all
classes of the great novelists of the nineteenth century has
outlasted Brecht's. Second, although Brecht's plays are more
accessible than the difficult masterpieces of modernism, there's
something unconvincing about his declaration that his
Lehrstücke were written for the 'workers' (they were, in fact,
written for working-class Communists). This cerebral, but
important debate took on perilous consequences in Stalin's
Russia, where any work that defied officially sanctioned forms
was condemned as counter-revolutionary and its leading figures
were silenced and persecuted.

The complexity of these arguments shouldn't deflect us from
appreciating the quality and nature of Brecht's 'realism'. The
simple fact is that Brecht shocked the European theatre by his
commitment to a working-class perspective on the world. No
playwright since Shakespeare (and possibly O'Casey, Lawrence
and Hauptmann) had given working people so central a role or
argued so consistently for their interests. It's a view that the
modern British theatre dispenses with at its peril.

▶ See Exercises 40, 41, 42, 43, 44 & 45 (Contradiction/
   Complex Seeing) and 19, 20, 21, 22 & 23 (Social
   Relationships)

The 'Merely Enjoyable'?

The reader of *A Short Organum for the Theatre* is often surprised by Brecht's declaration:

> Let us therefore cause general dismay by revoking our decision to emigrate from the realm of the merely enjoyable, and even more general dismay by announcing our decision to take up lodging there.[43]

Of course, Brecht understood that the 'merely enjoyable' has a serious role to play. He knew that nothing opens the mind as effectively as laughter and that only a relaxed audience member is capable of rethinking the familiar. But Brecht was also reacting against German culture's tendency for high seriousness and, crucially, understood that Teutonic solemnity could be antithetical to rational thought.

Pure pleasure is fundamental to many of the plays: sometimes – as in the high jinks in *Man Equals Man* or the black comedy of *Arturo Ui* – 'jolliness' is a cover for something much more sinister; at other times, as in *The Threepenny Opera* or *Mahagonny*, the pursuit of pleasure is central to the money-making machine of capitalism.

More positively, laughter is used as a weapon against the self-important posturing of those in power: the Merchant in *The Decision*, the Gods in *The Good Person of Szechwan* and the Very Old General in *Mother Courage* are good examples. And Brecht satirised Fascism in the same way: he pasted into his *Journals* a sequence of photographs of Hitler dancing like a hyperactive child (Chaplin's film *The Great Dictator* did the same), and a demystification of the dictator's buffoonery lies at the heart of *Arturo Ui*.

In later years, this emphasis on fun was replaced by the notion of 'cheerfulness', summarised brilliantly by Shen Teh:

> There are still friendly people, for all our wretchedness.
> When I was little once I was carrying a bundle of sticks
> and fell. An old man helped me up and even gave me a

penny. I have often thought of it. Those who have least to
eat give most gladly. I suppose people just like showing
what they're good at; and how can they do it better than
by being friendly? Crossness is just a way of being
inefficient. Whenever someone is singing a song or
building a machine or planting rice it is really
friendliness.[44]

Of course, the danger of such 'friendliness' can be seen in the
smiling peasants and cheerful workers of totalitarian propaganda, all happy to be pulling in the same direction for the good
of the country – and its dictator. On occasions, such as the Prologue to *The Caucasian Chalk Circle*, Brecht doesn't entirely
avoid this cliché; at its best, however, 'friendliness' celebrates
one of the key characteristics of shared problem-solving.

The lesson for the modern theatre is to encourage an
approach that is relaxed, intelligent and spirited. Even the most
serious of subjects should be presented with the suggestion that
they are temporary and subject to change. In our fatalistic times,
it's a brave position to take. But if you believe that injustice,
poverty and deprivation should be fought, only a theatre that is
enjoyable and fundamentally optimistic can help.

▶ See Exercise 34 (Stand -up Commentary)

The Lessons of Sport

One of the characteristics of many radicals of the 1920s and '30s
was an abiding interest in sport. Mass sporting events drew
large working-class crowds, featured athletes chosen for their
innate talents and strengths, not their background or education,
and promoted energy and physical prowess. The fact that many
people on the right were drawn to sport for the same reasons did
not deter its admirers on the left.

Brecht declared, 'We pin our hopes on the sporting public,'[45]
and sport helped him develop his new kind of popular theatre.
The Prologue to *In the Jungle of the Cities* announces that:

You are about to witness an inexplicable wrestling match
between two men and observe the downfall of a family that
has moved from the prairies to the jungle of the big city.
Don't worry your heads about the motives for the fight,
concentrate on the stakes. Judge impartially the technique
of the contenders, and keep your eyes fixed on the finish.[46]

Brecht enjoyed the clash between opposing forces, working
within clearly defined rules, but driven by grace, energy and
skill. And he was intrigued by the way that sports fans watch
their heroes: with passionate interest, certainly, but also with
critical detachment, not just caring about the outcome, but
assessing the skills used.

In Berlin, Brecht struck up a friendship with the heavyweight
boxer, Paul Samson-Körner, and Galy Gay in *Man Equals Man*
bears his nickname – 'The Human Fighting-Machine'. The soldiers in Brecht's famous production walked around on stilts and
Neher's sets for *The Little Mahagonny* employed a boxing ring
as its central metaphor; a similar emphasis can be detected in
the *Lehrstücke*. If, in later years, Brecht's interest in sport faded,
it was evident in the Ensemble's astonishingly athletic production of *Arturo Ui* after his death.

Sport has lost much of its subversive power. The last thirty
years have seen a number of plays about sportsmen, most of
which dramatise a rags-to-riches story of the working-class
sporting hero, but a new play about a Premier League footballer
is more likely to be a cautionary tale about giving a young lad
unimaginable wealth than an inspiring story of his struggle to
succeed against overwhelming odds.

Brecht's emphasis on sport is still useful in that it encourages
us to focus on the competition that lies at the heart of good
drama. It reminds us that society is built out of the struggle
between different forces, and that we can best understand the
way that the world changes when we grasp the clash of diametrically opposed energies.

▶ **See Exercise 12 (Sports Commentary)**

A Theatre for Smokers

In the 1920s, Brecht came up with the idea of a 'smokers' theatre' and, at one point, even declared:

> I even think that in a Shakespearean production one man
> in the stalls could bring about the downfall of western
> art. He might as well light a bomb as light his cigar. I
> would be delighted to see our public allowed to smoke
> during performances. And I'd be delighted mainly for the
> actors' sake. In my view it is quite impossible for the
> actor to play unnatural, cramped and old-fashioned
> theatre to a man smoking in the stalls.[47]

It's impossible to imagine this today, in our anti-smoking world, but it gives a sense of Brecht's hope that the spectator might watch the action with all the objectivity, scepticism and analytical skill of a chess player considering his opponent's latest move.

Photographs of Brecht often show him wreathed in tobacco smoke. Cigars, these photos suggest, allow the poor proletarian writer to partake of the exclusive luxuries of the rich. Cigars, he joked, were 'part of my means of production', and he smoked them throughout the HUAC hearings. One could say that his theatre is like his cigars: pungent, provocative and poisonous, but also stimulating, addictive and intensely pleasurable.

The 'Lehrstücke'

In the late 1920s, Brecht started to write a new kind of drama. Taking their inspiration from the oriental theatre – but also the great Bach Masses, German Romantic drama and modern popular culture – the Lehrstücke (best translated as 'learning plays') employ music, direct address and focused dramatic action to make their point. Intended for the participants (workers' choirs and amateur groups) as much as their audiences, these surprisingly sophisticated pieces are nothing less than an attempt to create a new kind of liturgical drama.

Although Brecht's dramatic style moved beyond the restraints of the *Lehrstücke*, their formal daring had a huge impact on his later work, and their legacy can be seen in his masterpieces. He even referred to them as the best possible model for the theatre of the future.

The eight *Lehrstücke* include two of Brecht's greatest works, *The Decision* and *The Mother*, which he described in some detail:

> *The Mother* is such a learning play, and embodies certain principles and methods of presentation of the non-Aristotelian, or epic style, as I have sometimes called it; the use of the film projection to help bring the social complex of the events taking place to the foreground; the use of music and of the chorus to supplement and vivify the action on the stage; the setting forth of actions so as to call for a critical approach, so that they would not be taken for granted by the spectator and would arouse him to think.

And he concluded:

> Briefly, the Aristotelian play is essentially static; its task is to show the world as it is. The learning play is essentially dynamic; its task is to show the world as it changes (and also how it may be changed).[48]

It's difficult to imagine the *Lehrstücke* making much of a comeback in the modern theatre. We claim to be too sophisticated to accept drama that tries to teach us, too ironic, if you like. But this is to underestimate the richness of the thinking in the *Lehrstücke* themselves, which explore complex questions of means and ends in trying to change society.

▶ See Exercises 13, 14, 15, 16, 17 & 18 (Argument and Clarity)

'Plays for Today'

The traditional, bourgeois defence of great art is that it gives voice to certain 'eternal truths' and provides insights into what it means to be human. As such, art is expected to speak to all people at all times, regardless of background, culture, religion or class.

Radicals, however, argue that claims of 'universality' simply negate the possibility of change. Human beings change according to their circumstances and Brecht's plays – especially those with the most direct political engagement – should be seen as products of their time, with particular relevance for particular circumstances. It was 'plays for the decade' that were needed, Brecht argued, not vain attempts at immortality. As a result, he added, they might have broad appeal:

> People are always telling us that we mustn't simply produce what the public demands. But I believe that an artist, even if he sits in strictest seclusion working in the traditional garret working for future generations, is unlikely to produce anything without some wind in his sails. And this wind has to be the wind prevailing in his own period.[49]

Only the writer engaged with the world can help to change it; we could add, ironically, that only then does his work stand a chance of speaking to future generations as well.

Of course, Brecht wasn't the first dramatist to address contemporary issues: Ibsen, Galsworthy, Shaw and Granville-Barker all shared the same ambitions. Our world has thrown up a vast range of new subjects – a global banking crisis, an economy in recession, international terrorism, climate change, and so on – and Brecht's commitment to 'plays for the decade' still offers a brilliant model for a modern politically engaged theatre.[50]

A Sense of History

The Marxist knows that the present is a product of the past and that it's impossible to create art that speaks to the modern world without some feeling for history. An understanding of Brecht's own work requires a grasp not only of the times in which he lived, but also of his own reading of the past. This drew from Hegel's theory of the dialectic, in which conflict between the classes leads inevitably – if often bloodily – to a better future. This belief in the possibility of progress does not exclude the tragic, but places the individual's experience within a broader context and sets personal suffering (the deaths of Pavel in *The Mother*, the Young Comrade in *The Decision* or Kattrin in *Mother Courage*) against the eventuality of a greater good.

As a result, ideas such as 'eternal truth' and 'human nature' are replaced by a concept of behaviour that is specific to environment. Brecht argued that a representation character that does not take into account the historical – and social – forces that have shaped it cannot be convincing, just as a story that does not refer to the specific conditions in which it occurs cannot be revealing. He insisted on 'playing things historically', and one of his key objectives was to show that the actions and arguments of the individual are a direct product of his historical moment. Walter Benjamin had argued that Fascism was 'a denial of history' and Brecht knew that progressive culture had to build on the lessons of the past.

Brecht was particularly interested in discovering those places in the drama – the 'useful junction points', as he called them – where the clash between periods and belief systems is most evident: the feudal and the modern in *Galileo*, or the bourgeois and the revolutionary in *The Mother*. Of course, this runs the danger of massive simplification, but highlighting these moments helps the audience see the drama historically, and places individual actions within a broader context, as part of a process of change.

'Playing things historically' is essential when approaching plays from the past. As Brecht argued, without a sense of history

we can never understand the particular nature of the problems
that face us today:

> When our theatres perform plays of other periods, they
> like to annihilate distance, fill in the gap, gloss over the
> differences. But what comes then of our delight in
> comparisons, in distance, in dissimilarity – which is at
> the same time a delight in what is close and proper to
> ourselves?[51]

▶ See Exercises 48 & 49

Theatre and Science

The Marxists see science as the best way of opposing the mys-
ticism inherent in organised religion and Fascism. So it's hardly
surprising that Brecht was eager to create a 'theatre for the scientific age'.

Brecht tried to show the complexities of 'the scientific age'
with the simplest of means. With the exception of *Saint Joan of
the Stockyards*, he wasn't particularly interested in portraying
the alienation caused by technology, or in celebrating the
advancement of science for its own sake. Instead, he wanted his
audience to learn the great lesson of science – the analytical,
evidence-based scientific method – and encouraged an approach
to social problems that was practical, rational and free of prior
assumptions.[52]

As Brecht's political analysis matured, he became increasingly
interested in discovering who would benefit from science's
advances: the rich and the powerful, or the poor and the
oppressed? Galileo's great speech of warning, written after the
dropping of the atomic bombs on Japan, gives a powerful sense
of Brecht's own concerns:

> You may in due course discover all there is to discover,
> and your progress will nonetheless be nothing but a
> progress away from mankind. The gap between you and
> it may one day become so wide that your cry of triumph

at some new achievement will be echoed by a universal
cry of horror.[53]

It's perhaps unsurprising that, in his last years, Brecht was contemplating a play about Albert Einstein.

Other dramatists have pursued similar connections, from
Karel Capek's play about robots, *R.U.R.*, to *Copenhagen*,
Michael Frayn's breathtaking dramatisation of 'chaos theory'.
The last thirty years have seen astonishing rates of scientific
advance, and modern drama should learn from Brecht's
attempts to discuss its implications.

'Play One Thing After Another'

Badly done, performances of Brecht's plays can feel inter-
minable and, certainly, the large-scale ones usually benefit from
careful cutting. But it's also a question of production style.

Brecht insisted that actors should 'play one thing after
another'. What he meant was a way of acting (and directing)
which presented the discrete moments of action for all their
worth, and didn't try to merge them together. He hoped that
such an approach would give the audience a chance to inspect
each moment individually and savour it for its content, instead
of being swept along uncritically by the action. He insisted that
actors should find detail in a vast collection of small social 'gests'
– paying the servants, bowing to royalty, serving at table, and so
on – which, taken together, offer a diagram of the way that the
society operates. It's an invaluable insight that should be applied
to all kinds of acting.

The danger, of course, is that it can slow the dramatic action.
But, done well, this sequence of individual actions is played fast:
the important thing is not to smooth them over. In a telling note
to the actors of the Berliner Ensemble on their first visit to London, Brecht wrote:

The English have long dreaded German art as sure to be
dreadfully ponderous, slow, involved and pedestrian...

So our playing must be quick, light and strong. By
quickness I don't mean a frantic rush: playing quickly is
not enough, we must think quickly as well. We must keep
the pace of our runthroughs, but enriched with a gentle
strength and our own enjoyment. The speeches should
not be offered hesitantly, as though offering one's last
pair of boots, but must be batted back and forth like
ping–pong balls.[54]

Anyone attempting to stage Brecht today should remember this.

▶ See Exercises 7, 8, 9, 10, 11 & 12 (Story and Narrative)
  and 17 & 18 (Speed, Lightness, and Fun)

Signs, Symbols and Written Texts

Brecht often used written texts in his productions: on hand-held
placards, on signs hanging from the flies, on symbols attached
to furniture or scenery. It's important to understand, however,
that such 'literalisation' is hardly ever used to express Brecht's
own beliefs: instead they provide a set of conflicting postures
which, taken together, help the audience deconstruct the texts
that shape society.

As a young man, Brecht loved the stalls at the Augsburg fair
with their graphic depictions of human failures, and borrowed
such moral tableaux – wickedness punished, goodness
rewarded, and so on – as a way of upending moral certainties
and creating new ones. He was also inspired by contemporary
fine art: the Cubists used newspaper cuttings, as did John
Heartfield (born Hertzfeld) in his political collages, and
quotations and references were fundamental to several
Modernist novels.

Brecht used this 'literalisation' in various productions:
Neher's provocative signs in *Drums in the Night*, the slogans in
Mahagonny, the placards in the *Lehrstücke*, the captions on the
curtain for *Galileo* in the US, and the location signs hanging
over the stage during *Mother Courage*.

Such techniques would have little impact today – where the materiality of the written word has become a post-structuralist (and apolitical) cliché – but the spirit of literalisation is still useful, even if we employ modern information technology instead of crudely painted canvas signposts to achieve it.

▶ See Exercise 28 (Silent Movie)

1.   *Brecht on Art and Politics* (2003).
2.   *Aesthetics and Politics* (1977).
3.   Meg Mumford, *Bertolt Brecht* (2008).
4.   Stephen Unwin, *Guide to the Plays of Bertolt Brecht* (2005); and 'Acting Brecht' in *Reacting: A Fresh Approach to Key Practitioners* (2008).
5.   'On Experimental Theatre' (1939–40).
6.   'A Short Organum for the Theatre'.
7.   *Ibid.*
8.   *Ibid.*
9.   'Alienation Effects in Chinese Acting' (1936).
10. 'Theatre for Pleasure or Theatre for Instruction' (c. 1936).
11. 'Short Description of a New Technique of Acting which Produces an Alienation Effect' (1940, pub 1951).
12. *Ibid.*
13. 'A Short Organum for the Theatre'.
14. 'Third Appendix to the Messingkauf Theory' in *The Messingkauf Dialogues*.
15. *Ibid.*
16. *Ibid.*
17. 'The Epic Theatre and its Difficulties' (1927).
18. 'On the Use of Music in an Epic Theatre' (1935).
19. 'Theatre for Pleasure or Theatre for Instruction' (1936?).
20. Walter Benjamin, *Understanding Brecht* (1998).
21. See, for example, 'The Modern Theatre is the Epic Theatre' (1930).
22. 'Theatre for Pleasure or Theatre for Instruction' (1936?).
23. 'The Epic Theatre and its Difficulties' (1927).
24. 'The Street Scene' (1938).
25. Walter Benjamin, *Understanding Brecht*.
26. 'On Form and Subject Matter' (1929).
27. 'The Question of Criteria for Judging Acting' (1931).
28. 'Indirect Impact of the Epic Theatre' (1935).
29. 'On Gestic Music' (1932?).
30. *Ibid.*
31. 'A Short Organum for the Theatre'.
32. *Ibid.*
33. *Ibid.*
34. *Ibid.*
35. 'The Film, the Novel and Epic Theatre' (1931).
36. Apparently, while directing *The Chalk Circle*, Brecht exasperated his colleagues by continually exposing the contradictions implicit in every decision – including his own – and challenging them accordingly.

37.   Appendices to the 'Short Organum'.
38.   *The Messingkauf Dialogues* (1965).
39.   'The Popular and the Realistic' (1937).
40.   *Ibid.*
41.   The key articles can be found in *Aesthetics and Politics.*
42.   'The Popular and the Realistic' (1937).
43.   'A Short Organum for the Theatre' (1948).
44.   *The Good Person of Szechwan.*
45.   'The Emphasis on Sport' (1926).
46.   *In the Jungle of the Cities* (1923).
47.   This is mentioned by John Willett in a note to 'Emphasis on Sport' in *Brecht on Theatre* and was probably written in 1922.
48.   'The German Drama: pre-Hitler' (1935).
49.   'Emphasis on Sport' (1926).
50.   Perhaps the most impressive recent manifestation of this has been the documentary plays presented at the Tricycle Theatre in Kilburn under the Artistic Directorship of Nick Kent.
51.   Appendices to 'A Short Organum'.
52.   Examples include: Galileo asking the professors to look through the telescope and make up their own minds, or Azdak awarding the child to the woman who is most evidently capable of caring for him.
53.   *Life of Galileo* (1958).
54.   *Letters.*

3

In Practice

3

In Practice

ACTING

The word 'Brechtian' has so often been used as an excuse for bad acting that I thought it might be useful to describe some of the things that Brechtian acting *isn't*, as a way of approaching (dialectically, of course) a better understanding of what it *is*. In brief, then, Brechtian acting shouldn't be:

- *Caricatured* Because of the tag 'political', it's sometimes thought that in Brechtian acting the working class should all be played as saints, the middle class self-satisfied, and the rulers monstrous. In fact, Brecht's fascination with contradiction means that Brechtian acting explores the different layers of human behaviour and shows how it's possible to be *both* a heroic scientist *and* a coward (Galileo), a victim of war *and* someone who lives off its proceeds (Mother Courage), a kindly aristocrat *and* a vicious landlord (Puntila), a friend of the poor *and* a judge with little respect for justice (Azdak). Brecht's realism precludes any possibility of caricature.

- *Long-winded* Brecht's emphasis on clarity and precision, as well as his insistence on social detail, has sometimes led actors to perform the plays in a ponderous fashion, over-deliberate and slow. Instead, Brecht expected his actors to act with lightness, quick-wittedness and a sense of pleasure in showing how the world works. He despised the pseudo–intellectualism of much German theatre, and mocked its self-indulgent tendencies.

- *Strident*   Mother Courage says that 'a short anger changes nothing but a long anger can change the world', and this sense of political anger – with injustice, exploitation, cruelty and war – underpins Brecht's greatest works and should inform the way that they're acted. But anger, Brecht knows, takes on many forms, and anger alone isn't enough to change things: you need to be strategic, sophisticated, witty, sly and so much else besides. Being strident – shouting and barking, self-righteous and pompous – is alien to Brechtian theatre, and should be avoided at all costs.

- *Unemotional*   Confronted with the dead body of her son and asked if she recognises him, Helene Weigel as Mother Courage shook her head grimly and denied all knowledge. But as the soldiers took the body away to be thrown into a ditch, she opened her mouth in a great silent scream. This is a perfect example of the kind of emotion required by Brecht: it's not enough to have 'feelings', the actor must show us how those feelings are affected by the social context in which they are found. If Mother Courage admitted to recognising her son, her livelihood would be destroyed and her life would be in danger. Brechtian acting draws on emotion constantly, but recognises that it's only one part of human experience and changes according to its context. Brecht just didn't want emotion to become the only point of acting.

- *Unrealistic*   Brecht's fascination with the oriental theatre and his habitual stripping of things down to their essence sometimes inspire a kind of acting which has very little relationship to observable human behaviour: sometimes grotesque, at other times

abstract, bad Brechtian acting is entirely unrealistic.
But Brecht wanted a kind of acting that drew from all
the material details of the world and was rich with
observation but – crucially – showed that society was
capable of being changed. The distinction needs to be
drawn between mere imitation of the surfaces of the
world, and a kind of art that engages its audience in a
discussion about how that world is organised. But it
cannot engage in that discussion unless it refers to the
material world every step of the way.

* *Solemn*   Brecht lived in a terrifying time – one of the
darkest in history – and he often lamented that under
the circumstances it was impossible for him to write
about the pleasures of the world. Two world wars,
three murderous dictatorships, world recession and
the division of Europe are hardly the stuff of light
comedy. But the extraordinary, heroic, thing is just
how much spirit Brecht brought to his writing, and
how little solemnity is required in acting them. His
plays are not escapist fantasies, but something much
more interesting than stern-faced solemnity is
required to act Mother Courage, Galileo or the Good
Person of Szechwan. An inner optimism – however
misguided – is the key: the world can always be
changed, and the actor needs to show that this is the
case. Solemnity is hardly the point.

* *Undercast*   Perhaps because of the emphasis on an
'ensemble' of actors working together to tell a story –
and because of the teaching of Brecht in schools and
colleges – it's sometimes assumed that Brechtian acting
should be in some sense second-rate, or amateur. In
fact, of course, the opposite is the case. Brecht worked
with some of the greatest actors of his time, and the
Berliner Ensemble at its best was a galaxy of stars.
Brecht on stage needs great acting if it is to work.

So what are the qualities of Brechtian acting?

- *Intelligent*   Brecht asks his actors to share his complex and often contradictory analysis of the world and to communicate it to the audience. This requires a level of intelligent engagement with the subject and a preparedness to share that with others. But it's essential to distinguish such intelligence from higher education or academic scholarship: it's a kind of relaxed but incisive awareness of the way that society operates, not a demonstration of arcane learning.

- *Ironic*   Irony is the signal tone of Brecht's writing: the irony that exposes the injustice and cruelty of the world with dry wit and tough satire. Acting in Brecht's plays requires similar levels of irony, which then support a fundamentally realistic, sceptical view of the world, and an acute awareness of dramatic irony – where the audience knows more than the character – is also essential.

  ▶ See Exercises 7 & 8

- *Provisional*   Brecht wanted his gravestone to say 'He made suggestions, others carried them out', and in this spirit he called his complete works *Versuche*, or 'attempts'. This sense of the provisional is fundamental to Brechtian acting, which constantly indicates that every emotion is relative, and that all conclusions are subject to contradiction. Above all, such acting indicates that everything is open to change, even opinions.

  ▶ See Exercises 35, 36, 37, 38 & 39 (Moments of Decision) and 40, 41, 42, 43, 44 & 45 (Contradiction/ Complex Seeing)

- *Observant*   Brechtian acting is built out of a series of observations taken from real life. Instead of creating a performance from his imagination, the Brechtian actor draws from the behaviour he sees all around him: 'This is how a man behaves when he is losing his house,' he seems to be saying to the audience, 'I've seen something like that on my street,' and so on. In some ways the approach is Stanislavsky's: the difference is that the Brechtian actor shows the audience the observation in an active fashion, while the Stanislavskian actor has a passive attitude to the audience and presumes that they must be interested.

▶ See Exercises 24, 25, 26, 27 & 29 (Gestus) and 2, 3 & 6 (Observation)

- *Elegant* In Brecht, the presentation of the action should have a certain grace, a stylish confidence, which appeals to the audience's own sense of pleasure and elegance. The common mistake is to imagine that Brechtian acting is scruffy or awkward: instead, even the direst situation is presented with a considerable degree of theatrical *joie de vivre*. The performance, then, draws attention to the actor's craft and helps us see that the events being presented can be changed.

- *Passionate* Brecht knew that thought and feeling are not polar opposites, and wanted a kind of acting that was passionate about thinking and thoughtful about passion. The separation of the brain and the heart is, Brecht argued, a peculiarly bourgeois and idealised concept: watch the way real people behave in real circumstances, and it's immediately clear that the two are inextricably linked. And so acting in Brecht needs to be driven by the passion that can change the world, even when informed by the intellect needed to understand what needs changing.

LANGUAGE

Start with the Poems

The English-speaking world has tended to focus on Brecht the playwright and overlooked his greatness as a poet. But Michael Hofmann has described him as the finest German poet of his time, and John Willett argued that the poems offered the best introduction to the plays. Certainly, reading Brecht's poems can help us understand his theatrical style.

The quality of the poems is difficult to describe. At their best, they have a flinty, epigrammatic quality. Philosophical in ambition, they go about their business by appealing to our physical and material sensations, not by complex intellectual games. They're not especially difficult to understand – certainly not in the way that T.S. Eliot or Robert Lowell can be – but they depend on the reader catching Brecht's particular tone of voice.

Two examples. The first is his (originally unpublished) response to the violent suppression of the 1953 workers' revolt in East Germany:

> After the uprising of the 17th June
> The Secretary of the Writers' Union
> Had leaflets distributed in the Stalinallee
> Stating that the people
> Had forfeited the confidence of the government
> And could win it back only
> By redoubled efforts. Would it not be easier
> In that case for the government
> To dissolve the people
> And elect another?[1]

This was intended as a cry of despair against rulers of all kinds, but especially the Communist government of the recently formed East Germany. But irony is essential: I once found myself defending Brecht against somebody who solemnly quoted it as evidence of Brecht's Stalinism and, indeed, read without irony, it's easily misunderstood.

Another, less contentious, example might be Brecht's great elegy to the challenge of his times, 'To Those Born Later':

You who will emerge from the flood
In which we have gone under
Remember
When you speak of our failings
The dark time too
Which you have escaped.

For we went, changing countries oftener than our shoes
Through the wars of the classes, despairing
When there was injustice only, and no rebellion.

And yet we know:
Hatred, even of meanness
Contorts the features.
Anger, even against injustice
Makes the voice hoarse. Oh, we
Who wanted to prepare the ground for friendliness
Could not ourselves be friendly.

But you, when the time comes at last
And man is a helper to man
Think of us
With forbearance.[2]

Read this poem aloud: it provides a perfect example of the demands of Brechtian acting. Without some sense of history, of the dark times through which Brecht and his generation lived, we to whom the poem is addressed – 'those who are born later', in fact – cannot possibly understand the poet's desire for a better future and the regret for the compromises that have necessarily been made in the past. Without a sense of historical context, the poem is meaningless; with it, it's a masterpiece.

The Language of the Plays

Turning to the plays themselves, with their tough subject matter, clear-eyed objectivity, and increasingly rational purpose, we sometimes forget the intensity of the poetic imagination that went into their creation. But they are astonishing feats of linguistic invention and our approach to theatre will be anodyne if we don't embrace his peculiar and potent verbal creativity.

Brecht's early Expressionist piece *Baal* brilliantly catches the life and death of a drifter and a social outcast:

> Baal! Brother! Come with me! Give it up! Out to the
> hard dusty highroad: at night the air grows purple. To
> bars full of drunks: let the women you've stuffed fall into
> the black rivers. To cathedrals with small, pale ladies: you
> ask, dare a man breathe here? To cowsheds where you
> bed down with the beasts. It's dark there and the cows
> moo. And into the forests where axes ring out above and
> you forget the light of day: God has forgotten you. Do
> you remember what the sky looks like? (*He spreads his
> arms.*) A fine tenor you've turned into! Come brother! To
> dance, to sing, to drink! Rain to drench us! Sun to scorch
> us! Darkness and light! Dogs and women![3]

This is written with a visionary intensity that German drama had not witnessed since Büchner's *Woyzeck* (1836).

By the time of the *Lehrstücke*, the language has changed completely, and is much more functional and to the point:

> I am quite ashamed to offer this soup to my son. But I've
> no dripping left to put in it, not even half a spoonful.
> Only last week they cut a kopeck an hour off his wages,
> and I can't make that up however hard I try. I know how
> heavy his job is, and how badly he needs feeding up. It is
> bad that I cannot offer my son better soup; he's young
> and has barely stopped growing. He is very different
> from his late father. He's always reading books, and has
> never found his meals good enough. And so he is getting
> more and more disconnected.[4]

It's important to recognise, however (not just in this slightly lumpy translation), that the language isn't 'naturalistic'. Brecht isn't attempting the rhythms of real working-class speech; he's trying to express a series of attitudes.

A more colloquial tone can be heard in the mature plays, such as this delightful speech by the milkmaid in *Puntila and his Man Matti*:

> Here's the sort of life I lead. Half past three I have to get
> up, muck out the cowshed and brush down the cows.
> Then there's the milking to do and after that I wash out
> the pails with soda and strong stuff that burns your hands.
> Then more mucking out, and after that I have my coffee
> but it stinks, it's cheap. I eat my slice of bread and butter
> and have a bit of shut-eye. In the afternoon I do myself
> some potatoes and put gravy on them, meat's a thing I
> never see, with luck the housekeeper'll give me an egg
> now and again or I might pick one up. Then another lot of
> mucking out, brushing down, milking and washing out
> churns. Every day I have to milk twenty-five gallons...[5]

Brecht's style changed through his career, and actors and directors need to respond to the individual qualities of the text and not imagine that there is one simply definable writing style throughout.

In acting these texts we need to find a way of speaking that allows its realistic detail to be vivid and clear, while celebrating its creative, stylistic aspirations. It's a formidable acting challenge.

Translating Brecht

Most people in the British theatre have little German and in reading or staging Brecht we are dependent on the translators.

Compare four different readings of the Recruiting Officer's speech that opens *Mother Courage*.[6] The first is by John Willett and is an intriguing mixture of the literary and the colloquial:

How can you muster a unit in a place like this? I've been
thinking about suicide, Sergeant. Here am I, got to find
our commander four companies before the twelfth of the
month, and people round here are so nasty I can't sleep
nights. S'pose I get hold of some bloke and shut my eye to
his pigeon chest and varicose veins, I get him proper
drunk, he signs on the line, I'm just settling up, he goes for
a piss, I follow him to the door because I smell a rat; Bob's
your uncle, he's off like a flea with the itch. No notion of
word of honour, loyalty, faith, sense of duty. This place has
shattered my confidence in the human race, Sergeant.[7]

The second is by Michael Hofmann and emphasises the quality of 'up-speak' he detects in Brecht's characters – that sense
of ordinary people using the language of their 'betters' to make
themselves sound impressive:

How do they expect me to raise an army in a place like
this? I tell you, Sergeant, it's enough to drive a man to
suicide. I'm supposed to have four platoons for the
Captain by the twelfth, and the people here are so
degenerate that I can't sleep at night. Finally I come up
with a man, I manage to avert my eyes from his pigeon
chest and his varicose eyes, I've got him good and drunk,
he's signed on the dotted line, I'm settling up with the
landlord, and he says I'm just popping out for a moment
and I follow him out the door, because I have a sense of
foreboding; and I'm right, he's off like a scratched louse.
There's nothing here about a man abiding by his word,
or any sense of honour and upstandingness. I think I've
lost all faith in humanity, Sergeant.[8]

The third is by Eric Bentley, Brecht's first English translator. It
has energy and sparkle, but is very American in its phrasing:

How the hell can you line up a squadron in a place like
this? You know what I keep thinking about, Sergeant?
Suicide. I'm supposed to knock four platoons together by

the twelfth – four platoons the Chief's asking for! And
they're so friendly around here, I'm scared to go to sleep at
night. Suppose I do get my hands on some character and
squint at him so I don't notice he's pigeon-chested and has
varicose veins. I get him drunk and relaxed, he signs on
the dotted line. I pay for the drinks, he stops outside for a
minute. I have a hunch I should follow him to the door,
and am I right? Off he's shot like a louse from a scratch.
You can't take a man's word any more, Sergeant. There's
no loyalty left in the world, no trust, no faith, no sense of
honour. I'm losing my confidence in mankind, Sergeant.[9]

The fourth is my own. It's as accurate as possible and takes
hardly any liberties. And it's the shortest (nine words less than
the German):

How are you meant to raise a unit around here? Sergeant,
I've been thinking about suicide. I've got to recruit four
platoons for the General by the twelfth but the people
round here are so nasty I can't sleep at nights. I finally
got hold of one, looked him over and pretended not to
notice he's pigeon-chested and has varicose veins, I had a
nice drink with him, he signed up, I pay for the
schnapps, he strolls off, I go to the door because I'm
worried: dead right, he's off like a scratched louse.
There's no loyalty, no truth, no faith, no honour.
Sergeant, I've lost my faith in humanity.

I leave others to comment on the quality of these different versions. But it's clear that the exceptionally rich texture of
Brecht's language is hard to render into actable English. The
temptation is to use a form of working-class argot ('How the hell
are you meant to find soldiers in a shithole like this…?'), which
underestimates the eloquence that Brecht's writing enjoys. But
the opposite – a highly artificial tone – doesn't work either.

Perhaps the single biggest challenge facing our work on
Brecht's plays is to develop a new set of accurate but speakable
translations that are appropriate for the twenty-first century.

MUSIC

Classical theatre used music extensively and it played an important role in Shakespeare and seventeenth-century drama. With the development of opera and neoclassical drama, however, music and drama became divorced from each other, and the restraints of nineteenth-century naturalism and the introverted seriousness of Expressionism found little space for musical drama. But Brecht was determined to exploit a whole range of musical forms for his new kind of popular political theatre.

Brecht loved music. As a young poet he entertained his friends singing songs on the guitar:[10] it was his first experience of public performance and the tradition of the troubadour lies at the heart of many of his ideas about the theatre. One of the most important things he took from the popular tradition was the central role played by music.[11]

Brecht was fortunate to work with four of the finest German composers of his generation. Each brought different qualities: Kurt Weill's catchy, jazzy, syncopated popularism was the secret behind Brecht's biggest hit, *The Threepenny Opera*; Hanns Eisler's highly politicised, neoclassical militant music was the perfect match for the *Lehrstücke*; Paul Hindemith wrote the most challenging music of the four (some would say the greatest); and Paul Dessau, the youngest and least demanding, wrote highly successful songs and incidental music for several of Brecht's mature productions.

Music plays a variety of roles in Brecht's theatre. It intensifies the emotions and drives the narrative on. But it also interrupts the flow of the action, provokes a fresh look at what is happening and distances the emotions in such a way that they are quotable and consumable. Thus, it provides an ironical commentary on the action, draws attention to sentimentality, horror, self-importance, and so on, and shows them up as stock responses which can be subjected to rational argument.

The distinctly Brechtian sound draws on the broadest possible range of influences – popular music and jazz, as well as folk elements and classical motifs – but the diversity of its origins is always clearly preserved. The orchestration is deliberately thin, and each instrument is clearly distinguishable from the other.

Brecht was suspicious of the 'beautiful voice' (*bel canto*) and his performers were expected to sing in such a way that the words of his songs came immediately to the fore. It's hardly surprising, therefore, that some of the most successful interpreters of Brecht's songs – Lotte Lenya, Robyn Archer, Ute Lemper – are not blessed with classical operatic voices. It's their commitment to the words (*'prima la parola'*, as the old opera saying has it) that counts.

Brecht insisted that the different musical sections should be separated from each other and from the action, and wanted them to be presented as clearly defined musical numbers, as this poem demands:

> Separate the songs from the rest!
> By some symbol of music, by change of lighting
> By titles, by pictures now show
> That the sister art is
> Coming on stage.[13]

He was reaching back to an earlier, pre-Romantic era of musical theatre, in which arias are clearly separated from recitative, and favourite numbers are inserted and repeated regardless of dramatic logic.[13]

Typically, Brecht's study of the classics informed his views about the future. And, as a result, music is central to Brecht's theatre to an extent unique in twentieth-century drama.

DESIGN

Brecht's theatre is created for the eye as well as the ear, the senses as well as the intellect. He had a keen interest in fine art, and his writing often expresses a powerful and highly original visual imagination. And one of the most distinct features of his productions was their exceptional beauty.

It's one of the paradoxes of Brecht's theatrical aesthetic that an artist who was interested in communicating ideas should have been obsessed with the visual. But this is more than a matter of mere aesthetics, it's part of a philosophical and political approach that emphasises the physical above the intellectual, the concrete above the abstract, and argues that nothing exists beyond the material.

Fine Art

The evolution of Brecht's visual style is typically eclectic. He was drawn to a vast range of classical artists, especially the earthy realism of Dutch and German art of the sixteenth and seventeenth centuries. Brecht (like his contemporary W.H. Auden)[14] was fascinated by Breughel's *Landscape with the Fall of Icarus*, which, he argued, embodied all the key elements of the 'alienation effect':

> Anyone making a profound study of Breughel's pictorial contrasts must realise that he deals in contradictions. In *The Fall of Icarus* the catastrophe breaks into the idyll in such a way that it is clearly set apart from it and valuable insights into the idyll can be gained. He doesn't allow the catastrophe to alter the idyll; the latter rather remains unaltered and survives undestroyed, merely disturbed.[15]

But Brecht was also interested in the contemporary fine arts and knew many of the most important German artists of the interwar years: the drawings of Käthe Kollwitz inform the world of *Drums in the Night*, the paintings and etchings of Georg Grosz and Otto Dix are the visual correlative of *The Threepenny Opera*, while the political collagist John Heartfield helped clarify Brecht's notions of the 'alienation effect' and the 'epic theatre'. And the clean lines of Walter Gropius's Bauhaus influence the *Lehrstücke*, just as Picasso's politically inspired figurative art echoed Brecht's own mature theatrical style – indeed, Picasso's dove of peace became the symbol of the Berliner Ensemble after the war.

Stage Design

Brecht enjoyed close relationships with three important stage designers. The most significant was Caspar Neher, a close friend since school days in Augsburg. They worked together through-out – though they were separated by the war – and Neher's designs include *The Threepenny Opera*, *The Mother*, *Puntila* and *Galileo*. Neher was instrumental in creating Brecht's instantly recognisable visual style. Karl von Appen, who designed *The Caucasian Chalk Circle*, and Teo Otto, who designed *Mother Courage*, built on Neher's remarkable innovations.[16]

In Brecht's theatre, the stage picture is made up of clearly defined – and very detailed – elements, often set against the emptiest of backgrounds. Elegantly presented and finely pro-portioned, each part of the stage picture is carefully chosen to present some crucial section of the story. Nothing is wasted and everything is expected to communicate crucial information. Furthermore, Brecht's designers wanted the audience to under-stand how the scenic elements had been constructed, and celebrated the materials used and the craftsmanship involved: whether beaten copper, worn timber, shining steel, or taut wires. And where decorative elements are used, they're quite evidently artificial.

People sometimes think that Brecht's rejection of nineteenth-century naturalism meant that his productions were abstract or empty of human detail. In fact, they frequently featured natu-ralistic elements – a fragment of wall, a door, a piece of furniture, and so on. The important point is that these are arranged in such a way that they tell the story and embody the dramatic action. Furthermore, they feel provisional and capa-ble of being changed – literally, by actors and technicians, but metaphorically also, by history and social change.

Brecht's designers sometimes went further and presented the stage simply as a stage, stripped of all scenery, with the actors visible throughout: 'The theatre,' he wrote, 'must acquire *qua* theatre the same fascinating reality as a sporting arena during a boxing match. The best thing is to show the machinery, the

ropes and the flies.'[17] Such an approach encourages the audience
to look imaginatively; but it also provokes them into thinking
critically. As ever, Brecht was inspired by Shakespeare's theatre,
which had no scenery as such, but relied on costumes and props
for its visual impact, and entered into an unspoken contract with
the audience about what the theatre could not show – and what
it could.

One of Brecht's most famous scenic innovations was the
'half-curtain'. This was a thin, white sheet hung on a wire running across the front of the stage, which fluttered shut at great
speed between scenes (with changes of scenery taking place
behind). Text was sometimes projected onto it, or an actor
would step forward and a song would be sung; the important
point was that it cut across the illusion of the previous scene and
wiped the slate clean for the new image which was about to be
drawn on it.

Brecht wrote about stage design on several occasions, including this remarkable eulogy for Caspar Neher:

The war separated
Me, the writer of plays, from my friend the stage designer.
The cities where we worked are no longer there.
When I walk through the cities that still are
At times I say: that blue piece of washing
My friend would have placed it better.[18]

Typically, the aesthetic is given a political perspective: Neher's
visual judgement is not just acute, it rallies opposition to
destruction and war.

Costumes, Properties and Furniture

The Marxist understands that people's behaviour and views are
shaped by the food that they eat, the furniture they sit on and
the clothes they wear. And so a central characteristic of Brecht's
theatre, especially the Berliner Ensemble, was the enormous
attention paid towards costumes, props and furniture.

This is not simply an aesthetic point. Brecht's plays are dependent on material objects to make their meanings concrete: Galileo teaching Andrea about the movements of the earth, the sun and the moon, with the help of a chair, an apple and a tooth-pick; Mother Courage haggling with the Cook over the price of a starved capon; or Azdak drawing a chalk circle on the floor and placing the child between his natural mother and the serving girl who has looked after him. 'The truth is concrete,' Hegel declared, and Brecht's theatre constantly demonstrates the meaning of the phrase.

Brecht became fascinated by the evidence of work, the patina of frequent use, and insisted that every prop, costume or item of furniture should carry a sense of how it has been used. Brecht elaborated on this in a poem in praise of Helene Weigel:

Just as the millet farmer picks out for his trial plot
The heaviest seeds and the poet
The exact words for his verse so
She selects to accompany
Her characters across the stage.
All selected for age, function and beauty
By the eyes of the knowing
The hands of the bread-baking, net-weaving
Soup-cooking connoisseur
Of reality.[19]

If at times Brecht's interest in the material became almost fetishistic in its intensity, it ensured that his productions were rich with history and flavour, realistic and meaningful throughout.

Lighting

Brecht loved brilliant white light. This gave his work great visual clarity, in which everything is held up for analysis, like a body on a dissecting table. He even used car headlights in his early productions and several of his productions with the Ensemble used white cycloramas to intensify this effect of brilliant whiteness.

Light served a political as well as an aesthetic purpose. By lighting the servant as brightly as the king, Brecht showed that there is no 'hierarchy of reality'. What's more, the bright lights keep the audience alert. One of his theatre poems expressed this vividly:

> Give us some light on the stage, electrician. How can we
> Playwrights and actors put forward
> Our images of the world in half darkness? The dim twilight
> Induces sleep. But we need the audience's
> Wakeful-, even watchfulness. Let them
> Do their dreaming in the light. That little bit of night
> We now and then require can be
> Indicated by moons or lamps.[20]

As so often, the Elizabethan theatre, open to the daylight skies, provided him with his inspiration.

Furthermore, in a way that many found shocking, Brecht asked for the source of the lights to be made visible:

> There is a point in showing the lighting apparatus
> openly, as it is one of the means of preventing an
> unwanted element of illusion; it scarcely disturbs the
> necessary concentration. If we light the actors and their
> performance in such a way that the lights themselves
> are within the spectator's field of vision we destroy part
> of his illusion of being present at a spontaneous,
> transitory, authentic, unrehearsed event. He sees that
> arrangements have been made to show something;
> something is being repeated here under special
> conditions, for instance in a very brilliant light.
> Displaying the actual lights is meant to be a counter to
> the old-fashioned theatre's efforts to hide them. No one
> would expect the lighting to be hidden at a sporting
> event, a boxing match for instance.[21]

Exposing the lights was anathema to the naturalistic theatre, but it's fundamental to the breaking of the illusion that Brecht regarded as essential to attracting his audience's critical attention. It has become pretty much standard practice in most European theatres as a result.

DIRECTING

With the possible exceptions of Peter Brook, no one has been as influential on the art of the modern theatre director as Brecht. Indeed, one could argue that Brecht has had a greater influence on directing than on any other aspect of the theatre.

Brecht and the Directors

Brecht wasn't the first playwright to be involved in staging his own plays. It's not known what Shakespeare said to his fellow actors, but it's hard to imagine him not explaining something of his dramatic intentions; Molière was a great leading actor and made the key decisions about the way that his plays were staged (and acted the leading roles); Ibsen worked as a director before he started to write plays; and Chekhov was involved in (and sometimes disagreed with) the way that Stanislavsky directed his work. Theatre directing is a recent phenomenon but the great dramatists have always cared about the practical issues of staging their plays.

Three directors had an important influence on Brecht. The first was Vsevolod Meyerhold, whose astonishing work in Soviet Russia explored the relationship between theatre and revolution. The second was the Austrian entrepreneur and *metteur en scène* Max Reinhardt, whose remarkable theatricality suggested to Brecht something of theatre's expressive range. The third was the left-wing German director Erwin Piscator, whose groundbreaking work at the Volksbühne in Berlin showed the young Brecht how the theatre could be made into a vital revolutionary art form capable of addressing the contradictions and challenges of the machine age.

From the outset, Brecht had strong views about directing and showed little respect for other directors who stood in his way. Ironically, he often co-directed his work, and enjoyed a long and productive relationship with the talented Erich Engel, whose technical facility was matched by Brecht's unique creativity. Indeed, Engel was responsible for finishing the work on Brecht's German-language production of *Galileo*, following Brecht's death.

With the formation of the Berliner Ensemble, Brecht assembled a group of remarkable assistant directors: Manfred Wekwerth, Peter Palitzsch, Benno Besson, Carl Weber and others. He used these young men as sounding boards for his ideas, often discussing in loud voices from the stalls the way that a scene should be performed, even as rehearsals were unfolding on stage, and actively engaging them in a continuous dialogue about the function of the theatre itself.

Brecht's directorial style was characteristically contradictory: on the one hand he was highly dictatorial, insisting on the detail of every point; on the other, he wanted a collective approach, and saw continuous discussion as not just the best way of making decisions, but fundamental to a genuinely dialectical approach to theatre. Some members of the Ensemble complained that Brecht's insistence on exploring dialectics and contradiction became quite maddening in his last years.

The Modern Brechtian Director

The modern theatre director, working in a Brechtian fashion, can use the full panoply of Brechtian techniques: the 'alienation effect', the 'epic theatre', acting with *gestus*, and the exploration of contradiction; he can emphasise pictorial clarity, use realistic elements in a way that recognises that their disposition is temporary, acknowledge the material facts of the theatre in the stage picture, and employ bright lights; and he can employ literal elements such as signs and placards, present the music in individual and separated numbers, and so on. All of this can be helpful.

But directing in a Brechtian way derives, above all, from an attitude to the material and to the theatre's role in society. If the director doesn't ask the right questions about the text and interrogate the content of the drama itself, the technical paraphernalia is best avoided. And so, in deciding to take up what I call 'the Brecht challenge', the modern director needs to make sure that he shares some of Brecht's sceptical, materialist and dialectical approach to the world.

So what can the young director learn from Brecht's approach? We could perhaps boil it down to five salient points:

1. *The emphasis on the story*   Remember that good drama shows the way that things change and that story is the best way of conveying this change. And so it's essential that you ensure that every twist and turn of the story – however minor – is laid out as clearly as possible and treat the telling of the story as your primary duty. But in doing so, you should try to resist simplifying the narrative and ensure that the audience sees the developments as a direct result of the dialectical process.

   ▶ See Exercises 7, 8, 9, 10, 11 & 12 (Story and Narrative)

2. *The importance of the social content*   Accept that human beings are the product of their environment and ensure that these factors are made clear. Avoid reducing the characters to simple psychological specimens, and insist instead that they are part of the complex web of social relations in which they live.

   ▶ See Exercises 19, 20, 21, 22 & 23 (Social Relationships)

3. *The centrality of conflict and contradiction*   Understand that human history is the story of continual conflict, and that society – and the individuals that make up that society – is rife with contradiction. Be diligent in

searching out the elements of conflict and
contradiction at all times. And instead of saying that a
character is 'x', you should show that he is made up of
both 'x' and 'y' and insist on the actor playing both.
What's more, rather than presenting events as natural
or inevitable, you can show how they are the direct
product of human agency – and so could have
unfolded differently.

▶ See Exercises 40, 41, 42, 43, 44 & 45 (Contradiction/
Complex Seeing) and 35, 36, 36, 37, 38 & 39
(Moments of Decision)

4. *The need to question the values implied by the text*
Ensure that the 'progressive' elements in a play are
fully articulated and communicate them to the
audience. Insist that the 'reactionary' elements (and
most old plays are a combination of the two) are either
presented as the pertaining historical conditions, or
rewritten to such an extent that a modern audience
cannot miss their implications. And expect your actors
to understand these issues and ensure that they act in
such a way that the audience can follow them.

▶ See Exercise 47 (Focus Group)

5. *The need for a dramatic vividness in the presentation of
this story*   Recognise that the human figure is at the
heart of the theatre and search out ways of
highlighting the impact of that figure in motion, and
in relationship to others. While you should avoid
grotesques, or vacuous theatricality, insist that the
presentation of the action has a real snap and energy
to it.

▶ See Exercises 24, 25, 26, 27, 28 & 29 (Gestus) and
19, 20, 21, 22 & 23 (Social Relationships)

STAGING BRECHT'S PLAYS TODAY

Brecht's theatrical theory is so often regarded as an independent area of study in its own right that we run the danger of forgetting that his ideas about the theatre were intended, above all, as a tool for working on his own remarkable, if highly idiosyncratic, plays.

Difficulties

Staging Brecht's plays today presents us with a number of real difficulties. The first is that they were written in response to very particular 'dark times', in conditions that don't exist any more. Thus, while we may well be plunging into recession, it's unlikely that we'll see anything like the economic catastrophe of the 1930s. And whereas the far right is making worrying progress, the emergence of a Fascist organisation that could seize power in the way that Hitler did is hardly credible. And although terrorism and unstable nation states pose a threat, a war of the nature that occurred twice within forty years in the first half of the twentieth century is beyond belief. The point, of course – as Brecht would have been the first to point out – is that the problems we face are different from those he faced: whether environmental disaster, the breakdown of social cohesion, or a population explosion, they require a new kind of drama. In other words (and Brecht wouldn't have taken this as an insult), Brecht's plays have, to an extent, become irrelevant.

The second challenge is that the political and social analysis on which so many of the plays rest is questionable. If Brecht had merely insisted that the world was badly organised and that a more equitable distribution of its resources would be advantageous, one would be hard pushed to find many people who opposed it. But the fact is that not only does Brecht object to the entire edifice of capitalism, he sees revolution as the only way of addressing the resulting injustice. What's more, he continuously identifies the contradictions within individuals that stop them from doing anything about their living conditions, whether it's

the passivity induced by religion, the limited horizons of economic self-interest, or the disabling vanity of small differences.
His plays include revolutionaries, but even there he seems more
interested in the tactical divisions they face than in showing their
efficacy as a mass movement. Brecht's recipes for change are
often negative: he takes the need for change – revolution, even –
for granted and asks why it's not more broadly felt.

The third challenge faced by anybody trying to stage Brecht's
plays is that it's necessary to understand Brecht's intentions
(what he is trying to show) in every scene, if we are to make
them work at all. Usually a playwright's intentions – his message – emerges through the action of the play; Brecht's
approach is much more conceptual and challenging. Thus, we
can only appreciate the first scene of *Mother Courage* when we
understand the direct link between Courage's eagerness to make
money out of the recruiters, and the loss to the war of her eld-
est son; more crucially still, we won't be able to make clear the
meaning of Kattrin's death if we don't understand that Brecht
wants us to reject her act of bravery (climbing onto the roof and
banging a drum to warn the inhabitants of Halle of an imminent
attack) as a piece of sheer folly which leads to her death. In other
words, Brecht is deliberately counter-intuitive – after all, the
'alienation effect' is all about making the familiar seem strange
– and we can only grasp the power and potential of these great
plays when our reading is informed by an understanding of his
intentions. One could describe this complex negativity as one of
Brecht's characteristic weaknesses. Brecht's defence, I think,
would be that only such a rigorous and dialectical approach is
capable of changing our views of the world.

Brecht's intentions have been frequently travestied in the
modern theatre and the result is worse than useless: a heroic
Mother Courage, a courageous Galileo, a wise Gruscha or a
noble Azdak. Brecht lacks the 'negative capability'[22] of Shakespeare, and actors, directors and designers need to listen to his
views with the utmost attention if they are to make any sense of
his plays on stage.

Aesthetic Challenges

A Brecht play presents the director and actor with aesthetic challenges too.

When confronted by the theoretical essays, the particularity of the playwright's intentions and the strangeness of some of the material, we can become so fascinated – or bemused – by the theatrical effects that we lose sight of the stories that the plays tell. Which is why we should be careful not to overstate Brecht's peculiarities, or imagine that his plays are abstract works with little relationship to everyday experience, and describe nothing to which we can relate. We should remember that Brecht's plays are stories about human beings, not mere exercises in theatrical practice.

The crucial point is this: so much has been written about the self-conscious artifice of Brecht's theatrical style that we forget the extent to which he was a realist, with an overriding commitment to presenting a truthful portrait of society. He was careful to make a distinction between realism and naturalism, and recognised that there are no absolute standards in aesthetic matters. But his encouragement of a critical attitude towards the society being presented shouldn't be mistaken for a lack of realism in his analysis of human affairs.

And so we need to ask many of the same questions of a Brecht text that we bring to all acting: Who is this character I am playing? How old is he? What is his job? How does he earn his living? What does he want, both in the immediate term (his objectives) and in the longer run (super-objectives)? And what stops him achieving his objectives (the obstacles)? We need to supplement these questions with broader ones: What time of day is it? What's the weather like? What is the social and historical context of the action? And so on.

All these Stanislavskian-type questions need to be answered with reference to the text and to the world of the play. If we then subject the results to the further rigours of Brecht's stated approach, we will produce something that may well succeed.

Suggestions

Striking an appropriate balance between these various imperatives can be difficult. But I think it's possible to stage Brecht
well in the modern theatre, if everyone involved remembers the
following:

1. *Brecht's intentions need to be understood*   If the actors
   perform with a clear understanding of Brecht's political
   and social purpose, from scene to scene and from
   moment to moment, they will inevitably produce the
   'alienation effect'. Thus a production of *Mother Courage*
   in which the leading actress refuses to acknowledge that
   Courage is a businesswoman as well as a mother, whose
   commitment to her business makes it impossible for her
   to protect her children, will fail to communicate the key
   point of the play; by contrast, a production of *The Good
   Person of Szechwan* which made it clear that the 'good'
   Shen Teh needs to become the 'bad' Shui Ta in order to
   survive stands some chance of showing an audience
   what the play is all about. Everybody involved needs to
   understand Brecht's intentions – his thinking about the
   world as much as his views on the theatre – if they are
   to stage the plays at all.

2. *The plays are about human beings*   Brecht's plays tell
   stories about human beings in real situations. *Mother
   Courage* shows the price one particular woman pays in
   order to survive the desperate conditions of the Thirty
   Years War; *Galileo* shows how a great scientist operates
   within a society whose powerful forces are opposed to
   scientific progress; *The Mother* shows how a working-
   class woman joins the revolutionary cause. Each of
   these 'epics' is packed with 'dramatic' episodes.

3. *The value of realism*   Although Brecht's plays benefit
   from the chief features of the dramatist's theatrical
   style, a production needs to bring a level of social

realism and psychological insight, as well as emotional and dramatic commitment, if it is to communicate its chief points. The danger in modern productions is that they become a demonstration of Brechtian style, not a genuine attempt to present the particular drama that Brecht offers us.

A Note on the Model Books

Brecht recognised that his plays were difficult to stage and, following his return to Berlin, established the practice of producing 'model books': carefully documented accounts of the Berliner Ensemble's chief productions,[23] consisting of an extensive photograph record of every scene, and a range of incidental notes by Brecht and his associates. They're difficult to get hold of nowadays,[24] but most of the texts are featured in the Methuen editions of the plays.

The model books were created to give directors insights into the thinking behind his plays and their productions. Brecht was aware that they could be seen as constricting.[25] But the point is that the plays were written to be performed in a very particular way, and their meaning is only released when the author's theatrical intentions are understood. The model books offer invaluable insights, which a good director will find useful, even if just as a way of developing his own ideas.

BRECHT ON SHAKESPEARE

I first read Brecht at university. I was fortunate to have been taught by Margot Heinemann, and her lectures on Brecht and Shakespeare have shaped my approach to both writers ever since.[26] I've applied Brecht's approach in a dozen Shakespeare productions and the notes that follow are borne out by practical experience.

Brecht was obsessed with Shakespeare and a full-length study of his many (typically contradictory) insights is long overdue.

Much of the original material can be found in the letters, poems, journals and essays, as well as in his adaptation of *Coriolanus*, but nowhere does he talk about Shakespeare's theatre more fully than in *The Messingkauf Dialogues* – an extraordinary dramatised debate between a Philosopher, a Dramaturg, an Actor, a Technician and others, about art, politics and the theatre – and many of the insights that follow are drawn from them.

Historical Context

Like many Marxists, Brecht saw Shakespeare's England as the crucible of the modern world, and he was fascinated by the clash of forces (the feudal and the democratic, barter and trade, the country and the city) that shaped the period. This 'changing world'[27] was, he felt, the essential context for the great drama of the time.

In discussing Shakespeare, Brecht's Philosopher emphasises the importance of having some understanding of this:

> What really matters is to play these old works historically, which means setting them in powerful contrast to our own time. For it is only against the background of our time that their shape emerges as an old one, and without this background I doubt if they could have any shape at all.[28]

It's important to understand, however, that this emphasis on historical context means more than costume and setting: it's an acknowledgment of the historical processes that are embodied in the plays. Thus, the Brechtian would argue, we can only understand *Richard II* if we recognise the conflicting views of the 'divine right of kings' in a country which, fifty years later, would execute its monarch by Act of Parliament; and the first scene of *Coriolanus* (1608?) suddenly comes to life if we remember the rage and violence that characterised the Midland Revolt of 1607. Rather than pushing the plays back into mere scholarship, historical context can help bring the plays to life.

As a materialist, Brecht knew that much could be learnt from the original 'means of production':

> Plays were beginning to be treated as merchandise, but the conditions which governed property were still chaotic. Neither thoughts nor images, incidents, inspirations, discoveries were protected by law; the theatre was a source of discovery that was just like life.[29]

And although his scholarship is a little shaky, Brecht's assertions about Shakespeare's working conditions are revealing:

> Nothing gives a better idea of the sober, healthy, profane state of the Elizabethan theatre than a look at Shakespeare's contracts with his companies, which guaranteed him a seventh part of the shares and a fourteenth part of the income of two theatres; at the cuts he made in his own plays, amounting to between a quarter and a third of all the verses; at his instructions to his actors in *Hamlet* to act in a restrained and natural manner.[30]

In other words, Brecht argued, Shakespeare wrote for a commercial theatre and an embrace of the reality of the theatrical hurly-burly acts as a corrective to the Romantic view of the isolated genius.

Furthermore, Brecht argued that the physical realities of Shakespeare's theatre could help us understand his dramatic style:

> Add to that the fact that they acted (and also rehearsed, of course) by daylight in the open air, mostly without any attempt to indicate the place of the action and in the closest proximity to the audience, who sat on all sides, including on the stage, with a crowd standing or strolling around, and you'll begin to get an idea how earthly, profane and lacking in magic it all was.[31]

When the Actor says that he is worried about the possibility of 'illusion' in a theatre such as this, the Dramaturg is clear: 'People were supposed to use their imaginations.'[32]

Brecht celebrated the unique combination of high and low, rough and sophisticated, educated and popular, that is such a characteristic of Shakespeare's theatre, and argued that this mongrel quality was fundamental to its greatness:

> Its great personalities are its low personalities polished up; its high-bred speech is vulgar speech refined. How much was concessions to the educated public in the boxes; how much concessions to the pit? Colleges depended on beer gardens and beer gardens on colleges.[33]

The impurity of the whole undertaking is what attracts Brecht most. And this understanding of historical and theatrical context – however sketchy – provided Brecht with rich inspiration for the development of his own theatrical style.

The Limits of Empathy

Brecht knew that nineteenth-century notions of dramatic empathy are alien to Shakespeare's theatre:

> Take the element of conflict in Elizabethan plays, complex, shifting, largely impersonal, never soluble, and then see what has been made of it today, whether in contemporary plays or in contemporary readings of the Elizabethans. Compare the part played by empathy then and now. What a contradictory, complicated and intermittent operation it was in Shakespeare's theatre![34]

He also realised that the dynamic nature of this drama, with its overarching emphasis on narrative, inhibits simple empathy and stresses, instead, change and development:

> We grasp the old works by a comparatively new method – empathy – on which they rely little. Thus the greater part of our enjoyment is drawn from other sources than those which our predecessors were able to exploit so fully. We are left safely dependent on beauty of language, on elegance of narration, on passages which

stimulate our own private imaginations; in short, on the incidentals of the old works. These are precisely the poetical and theatrical means which hide the imprecision of the story. Our theatres no longer have the capacity to tell these stories, even the relatively recent ones of the great Shakespeare, at all clearly, i.e. to make the connection of events credible. And according to Aristotle – and we agree there – narrative is the soul of drama.[35]

Brecht then claimed that the 'alienation effect', with its continuous checking of empathy, is the inevitable result of an approach to old plays with a sense of history and society:

If we ensure that our characters on the stage are moved by social impulses and that these differ according to the period, then we make it harder for our spectator to identify himself with them. He cannot simply feel: that's how I would act, but at most can say: if I had lived under those circumstances.[36]

In other words, in such a theatre we are encouraged to look at what is presented with some degree of objectivity and analysis.[37]

A common mistake is to imagine that such a theatrical style is in some sense cold or lacking in human feeling. Margot Heinemann nails the lie:

It's not a question of eliminating feeling from the theatre. Empathy is only one kind of feeling, and not, says Brecht, one that the Shakespearean drama itself (as distinct from its modern interpreters) relies on much. Shakespeare's theatre was more concerned with telling stories, whereas modern interpreters are no longer interested in making the sequence of events credible and concentrate on making us share the inner life of the characters. Empathy in Shakespeare's theatre was a contradictory, complicated, intermittent operation: now it is taken as central.[38]

It's not a question of *either* feeling *or* thought: Brecht, like Shakespeare, expected both in continuous conversation with each other.

Importance of Relative Qualities

The Marxist knows that human beings are best understood when placed in relationship with others and their historical circumstance. And such relativism makes for the illusion of three-dimensionality in characterisation and the depiction of society. To the Actor's horror, the Philosopher and the Dramaturg point to the same quality of relativism in Shakespeare:

THE ACTOR: If I show a man as relatively ambitious nobody's likely to go along with it in the same way as if I showed him wholly and utterly ambitious.

THE PHILOSOPHER: But in real life people are more often relatively ambitious than wholly and utterly ambitious, aren't they?

THE ACTOR: Maybe. But it's a question of what's effective.

THE PHILOSOPHER: You must achieve that with something that's less unlikely to happen in real life. That's your business.

THE ACTOR: A nice Macbeth that would make: sometimes ambitious and sometimes not, and only relatively more ambitious than Duncan. And your Hamlet: very hesitant, but also very inclined to act too hastily, no? And Clytemnestra, relatively vindictive. Romeo, relatively in love...

THE DRAMATURG: Yes, more or less. You needn't laugh. In Shakespeare he's already in love before he's seen his Juliet at all. After that he's more in love.

THE ACTOR: Ha, a bursting scrotum! As if other people didn't suffer from that besides Romeo, and without being Romeos.

THE PHILOSOPHER: All the same, Romeo has got one. It's one of Shakespeare's great realistic strokes to notice that.

THE ACTOR: And Richard III's unholy fascination: how can I show that except by making it fill the whole of the character?

THE DRAMATURG: You mean in the scene where he so fascinates the widow of the man he's murdered that she becomes his victim? I can see two solutions. Either she must be shown to be terrified in to it, or else she must be made to be ugly. But however you show his fascination it won't do you any good unless you can show how she fails him later in the play. So you have to show a relative power of fascination.[39]

The Actor, with his addiction to intoxicating emotions, cannot accept that realistic drama shows people in relationships with others. But this relativity is fundamental to Brecht's 'epic theatre' and to any production of Shakespeare's that strives for social and psychological realism.

'Barbaric' Plays?

Much as he admired Shakespeare's dramatic technique, Brecht was sceptical about the eternal value of his plays. Echoing Walter Benjamin's famous dictum that 'There is no document of civilisation which is not at the same time a document of barbarism',[40] Brecht's Philosopher calls Shakespeare's plays 'barbaric'.[41] He wanted his audience to explore the extent to which the plays are stuck in their historical moment, but also where they look forward to more modern times.

For Brecht – and other Marxists – thinking historically means thinking dialectically. And so he came up with the concept of 'useful junction points' in Shakespeare, moments in the action when the clash of the conservative and the progressive, the reactionary and the revolutionary, are most in evidence. He wanted productions to point these moments up and show the way the different forces are in dramatic opposition to each other.[42] He even wanted such contrasts to be brought about through the deliberate exploitation of stylistic inconsistencies.

The Dramaturg is worried that such an approach will destroy the smooth fabric of the play. But the Philosopher is unimpressed:

Perhaps it does lead somewhere; we'd have to look at the play. In any case, it wouldn't hurt if there were some abnormal episodes of this sort, hotbeds of inconsistency that one suddenly stumbled into. The old reports are full of such things... And there are those useful junction points in his works where the new collided with the old. We are too at one and the same time fathers of a new period and sons of an old one.[43]

Of course, Brecht argued that these 'barbaric' plays sometimes need wholesale rewriting, or at least reconfiguring, if they're to be made relevant to modern circumstances:

THE DRAMATURG: Have we got to scrap all those marvellous old plays, then?

THE PHILOSOPHER: I wouldn't say so.

THE ACTOR: What about *King Lear*?

THE PHILOSOPHER: It's partly a report on the way people lived together in a previous age. All you've got to do is put the report into effect.

THE DRAMATURG: A lot of people think such plays ought to be performed as they stand, and claim that it would be barbarous to make any change in them.

THE PHILOSOPHER: But it's a barbaric play. Of course, you need to go about it very carefully if you're not going to spoil its beauty.

The point is that all kinds of updating, rewriting and repositioning are possible so long as we are engaged with the substance of the play, and are not merely tampering with the outward form. As Brecht said, 'We can change Shakespeare, if we can change him!'

Margot Heinemann was characteristically wise on the subject:

It's not enough if the director transits something like
the original production or throws light on the age when
the play was written; it has to say something meaningful
to modern spectators, not just to be part of a
respectable cultural heritage. But to modernise
effectively is not simple. It's not just a matter of
dressing Hamlet in a dinner jacket or Caesar in
Wilhelmine uniform, which merely introduces a
different set of anachronisms.[44]

Such a complex, dialectical approach can be usefully contrasted
to Jan Kott's[45] (and his many followers in the modern theatre),
which values the plays today only to the extent to which they
can be claimed as being 'contemporary'.

Brecht came to recognise that Shakespeare's plays can be performed with minimal changes, so long as they are staged with
'alienation', which, Brecht's Dramaturg says, will 'encourage the
audience to keep their heads':

> What you cannot have is the audience, including those who
> happen to be servants themselves, taking Lear's side to such
> an extent that they applaud when a servant gets beaten for
> carrying out his mistress' orders as happens in Act One,
> Scene Four.
>
> THE ACTOR: How are you to stop it?
>
> THE DRAMATURG: Say he was beaten and injured, then
> staggered with every sign of having been hurt. That would
> change their attitude.
>
> THE ACTOR: Then you'd have people turning against Lear for
> reasons associated with purely modern times. '
>
> THE DRAMATURG: Not if you're consequential about it. The
> servants of this generally unwanted king could be shown as
> a little group which no longer gets its meals anywhere and
> pursues him with dumb reproaches. Lear would have to
> wince at the sight of them, and that would be a good
> enough reason for him to lose his temper. You just have to
> show the feudal conditions.

THE ACTOR: In that case you might as well take his division of
his kingdom seriously and have an actual map torn up in
the first scene. Lear could hand the pieces to his daughter
in the hope of ensuring their love that way. He could take
the third piece, the one meant for Cordelia, and tear that
across once again to distribute to the others. That would
be a particularly good way of making the audience stop
and think.[46]

The underlying aim is – as ever – finding ways of encouraging
the audience to look critically at the action.

Brecht came to appreciate the tremendous sophistication of
Shakespeare's dramatic technique, which, he acknowledged, was
capable of catching the 'truth of life'. It's perhaps telling that,
after a lifetime struggling with the question of how to stage
Shakespeare in the modern world, Brecht's last entry in his
Journals acknowledged that it would be 'possible to stage *Coriolanus* as it is, with good direction'.[47]

Shakespeare's Realism

At the heart of Brecht's work on Shakespeare was his apprecia-
tion of the quality of realism in the writing:

It's already impossible to perform these medieval plays to
audiences that don't have any historical sense. That's
sheer folly. But Shakespeare is a great realist, and I think
he'd stand the test. He always shovels a lot of raw
material on to the stage, unvarnished representations of
what he has seen.[48]

Of course, Brecht isn't talking about mere naturalism here: it's
an approach to the world which is sceptical, materialist and,
above all, dialectical. And this sense of 'raw material' – life that
refuses to be tidily categorised or fitted into simplistic intellectual or artistic categories – helps us appreciate the sheer
diversity and richness of the plays.

Here, as Margot Heinemann said, 'the acid test for a production that has assimilated the most important elements of

Brecht's thinking is how it deals with crowds, servants and the lower orders generally'. The 'common people' are crucial to Brecht's approach:

> In Shakespeare's own theatre, the common people must have been immediately recognisable by their dress, and by vernacular idiom and local dialect, in contrast to the elevated speech of aristocratic heroes. And they are, of course, often given the most searching comments on the heroic action. The Gravediggers, Pompey the bawd, the soldiers before Agincourt represent one of the most important means of distancing the main action and enabling the audience to judge it. Often, however, in modern productions these characters are routinely presented as gross, stupid and barely human – rogues, sluts and varlets with straw in their hair, whose antics the audience can laugh at but whose comments it can't be expected to take seriously.[49]

Of course, a similar emphasis on realism could be extended to the aristocratic characters: an approach which understands class and acknowledges social difference is also much more dramatic.

The extraordinary range of Shakespeare's dramatic style inspired Brecht's own 'epic theatre':

> With Shakespeare the spectator does the constructing. Shakespeare never bends the course of human destiny in the second act to make a fifth act possible. With him everything takes its natural course. In the lack of connection between his acts we see the lack of connection in a human destiny, when it is recounted by someone with no interest in tidying it up so as to provide an idea (which can only be a prejudice) with an argument not taken from life. There's nothing more stupid than to perform Shakespeare so that he's clear. He's by his very nature unclear. He's pure material.[50]

Thus, at the heart of Brecht's approach to Shakespeare is a new definition of 'realism': an approach to life more than an artistic genre or single convention. The theatre of the 'great realist', in other words, is dynamic and free-ranging, open-ended and diverse, and is the best kind of theatre to help us understand – and, as Brecht would hope, change – the world.

Classical Status as an Inhibiting Factor

Brecht recognised the very real danger in approaching classical theatre – especially Shakespeare, but other writers too – with such reverence that we are numbed into unthinking blandness. At the same time, he understood that the great plays of the past should be approached with care. In one of his most incisive essays, he wrote about what he called 'the ghastly boredom of traditional productions' of the classics, declaring:

> Actors and producers, many of them talented, set out to remedy this by thinking up new and hitherto unknown sensational effects, which are, however, of a purely formalist kind: that is to say, they are forcibly imposed on the work, on its content and on its message, so that even worse damage results than with traditional-style productions, for in this case message and content are not merely dulled or flattened out but absolutely distorted. Formalist 'revival' of the classics is the answer to stuffy tradition, and it is the wrong one. It is as if a piece of meat had gone off and were only made palatable by saucing and spicing it up.[51]

It's still relevant, when productions of Shakespeare are often innovative and theatrically exciting, but lacking in any social, political or historical insight. We need to pay attention to the 'meat'.

Summary

We can summarise (if also simplify) Brecht's approach to Shakespeare in the following five points of advice to anyone trying to stage the plays today:

- Remember the historical context, especially the contradictions of the period, and do everything you can to dramatise them as vividly as possible.

- Question the underlying assumptions both in the play and in the way that it has been received. Approach the material with a mixture of scepticism and care, radical intervention and historical objectivity. Let your work be contradictory.

- Emphasise narrative above all. Be careful not to substitute dynamic change with a flattening statement of the play's 'meaning'. In other words, respect the dialectic and bring out the clash of historical forces that shape the dramatic action.
  ▶ See Exercises 7, 8, 9, 10, 11 & 12 (Story and Narrative)

- Employ the simplest of dramatic means to tell the story, and perform with a free and relaxed relationship with the audience and a continuous awareness of what is being shown.

- Present characters with a high degree of dynamic realism, shaped by social circumstances as much as psychological factors. Understand the need for a 'relative' approach to characterisation, and pay attention to the three-dimensional reality of the working people. Embrace the way that Shakespeare seeks empathy for his characters one minute, and the next provokes critical objectivity.
  ▶ See Exercises 19, 20, 21, 22 & 23 (Social Relationships)

One could add the value of a 'gestic' approach to speaking the text, the use of a clear, open platform on which to present a continuously changing set of social relations, an acceptance of the disjunctions inherent in the text and an attention to the changing social and class structures that underpin the dramatic action.

▶ See Exercises 24, 25, 26, 27, 28 & 29 (Gestus)

1. 'The Solution', *Poems 1913–1956*.
2. 'To Those Born Later', *Poems 1913–1956*.
3. *Baal*, translated John Willett.
4. *The Mother*, translated John Willett.
5. *Puntila*.
6. The original German is: 'Wie soll man sich hier ein Mannschaft zesammenlesen? Feldwebel, ich denk schon mitunter an Selbstmord. Bis zum Zwölften soll ich dem Feldhauptmann vier Fähnlein hinstelln and die Leut hier herum sind so voll Bosheit, daß ich keine Nacht mehr schlaf. Hab ich endlich einen aufgetrieben und schon durch die Finger gesehn und mich nix wissen gemacht, daß er ein Hühat and Krampfadern, ich hab ihn glücklich besoffen, er hat schon unterschrieben, ich zahl nur noch den Schnaps, er tritt aus, ich hinterher zur Tür, weil mir was schawnt: richtig, weg ist er, wie die Laus unterm Kratzen. Da gibts kein Manneswort, kein True and Glauben, kein Ehrgefühl. Ich hab hier mein vertrauen in die Menscheit verloren, Feldwebel.'
7. *Mother Courage*, translated John Willett.
8. *Mother Courage*, translated Michael Hofmann.
9. *Mother Courage*, translated Eric Bentley.
10. A friend of Brecht's later recalled: 'He did not sing in a polished way, but with a passion that swept others along, drunk from wine and his singing made those who heard him drink also'. Brecht can be heard singing 'Mack the Knife' on Alex Ross's remarkable website: http://www.therestisnoise.com/2007/01/chapter-6-city-.html
11. Bob Dylan, perhaps Brecht's most natural poetic successor, cites Brecht's songs as central to his inspiration. See Bob Dylan, *Chronicles* (2004).
12. 'The Songs', *Poems 1913–1956*.
13. 'On the Use of Music in an Epic Theatre' (1935).
14. W.H. Auden's poem 'Musée des Beaux Arts' (1938) is a meditation inspired by Breughel's painting, *Fall of Icarus*, which – quite independently – describes the essential features of the 'alienation effect' and 'complex seeing'. The first four lines establish the argument:

> About suffering they were never wrong,
> The Old Masters: how well they understood
> Its human position; how it takes place
> While someone else is eating or opening a window or just walking
>   dully along

15. See 'Alienation Effects in the Narrative Pictures of the Elder Breughel' (1934).

16. John Willett's *Caspar Neher, Brecht's Designer* (1986) reproduces the most important drawings, but a full-length monograph in English is long overdue. No books in English on Karl von Appen or Teo Otto are currently available.
17. 'Short Description of a New Technique of Acting' Appendix (1940).
18. 'The Friends', *Poems 1913–1956*.
19. 'Weigel's Props', *Poems 1913–1956*.
20. 'The lighting', *Poems 1913–1956*.
21. 'Short Description of a New Technique of Acting which Produces an Alienation Effect' (1940).
22. John Keats, *Letters*.
23. Model books exist of *Antigone* (1948), *Señora Carrar's Rifles* (1952), *Life of Galileo* (1958) and *Mother Courage* (1958).
24. A few years ago I managed to buy a copy of the *Mother Courage* model book on the internet.
25. See 'Does Use of the Model Restrict the Artist's Freedom?'.
26. Heinemann's chapter 'How Brecht Read Shakespeare' in *Political Shakespeare* (1985) is hard to better.
27. See Arnold Kettle's important collection of essays, *Shakespeare in a Changing World* (1964).
28. *The Messingkauf Dialogues*.
29. *Ibid.*
30. *Ibid.*
31. *Ibid.*
32. *Ibid.*
33. *Ibid.*
34. 'A Little Private Tuition for my friend Max Gorelik' (1944).
35. 'A Short Organum for the Theatre'.
36. *Ibid.*
37. Brecht even called Shakespeare's theatre 'a theatre full of alienation effects!' (see page 24).
38. Margot Heinemann, 'How Brecht read Shakespeare', in *Political Shakespeare*.
39. *Ibid.*
40. Walter Benjamin, *Theses on the Philosophy of History* (1940).
41. *Short Organum for the Theatre* (elsewhere, Brecht describes them as 'drama for cannibals', adding, 'We know that the barbarians have their art. Let us create another').
42. Two examples of this: the moment when Theseus in *A Midsummer Night's Dream* (4.1) overrules his courtier Egeus with his demand for punishment of his disobedient daughter and lover Lysander; the episode in which an anonymous servant kills the Duke of Cornwall in *King Lear* (3.7), and launches the opposition to tyranny.

43. *Ibid.*
44. Margot Heinemann, 'How Brecht read Shakespeare', in *Political Shakespeare.*
45. Jan Kott (1914–2001) was a distinguished Polish academic, whose views were formed in the Nazi occupation and under Communism. He saw Shakespeare as a writer whose plays could provide a mirror image to his own time and preoccupations. His book *Shakespeare Our Contemporary* (1964) was one of the most influential works of Shakespearean criticism of the twentieth century. He draws fascinating parallels between his world and Shakespeare's. The great value of Kott's approach is that such startling juxtapositions reveal new insights into the action. They impart to the text an energy which gives them urgency and immediacy. For all its attractions, however, Kott's approach causes as many problems as it solves. The first is that it emphasises the single image at the expense of the story. Kott discovers resonance, and even relevance, in the isolated moment, but cannot sustain it in the dramatic action: the icon replaces the story, and dynamic change is ignored in favour of the static picture. Furthermore, Kott fails to recognise Shakespeare's respect for – and interest in – history. By denying the particular nature of history and preferring to emphasise the repetitive and cyclical pattern of what he calls the 'Grand Mechanism' of murder and assassination, Kott neglects Shakespeare's grasp of historical process and social change altogether. The most significant problem is that Kott ignores the particular context in which the action of the plays take place: violence, cruelty, appetite, ambition and greed may recur throughout human history, but their significance is different according to the circumstances in which they appear. By fusing the past with the contemporary, Kott does an injustice to both. It's entirely different from Brecht's approach.
46. *The Messingkauf Dialogues.*
47. *Journals 1934–1955.*
48. *The Messingkauf Dialogues.*
49. Margot Heinemann, 'How Brecht read Shakespeare', in *Political Shakespeare.*
50. 'Introduction to *Macbeth*' on Berlin Radio (1927).
51. 'Classical Status as an Inhibiting Factor' (1954).

4

The Brecht Challenge

4

The Brecht Challenge

THE CHALLENGE

Brecht sets the modern theatre artist a tough challenge. It's hard enough to create a kind of theatre that reflects the reality of the world, but persuading the audience to criticise that reality, as Brecht wanted them to, is much, much harder. We can reject both objectives if we wish and declare that the theatre exists simply for fantasy and escapism. But once we declare our commitment to its role as a teller of truths, and as something that can play an active role in improving the way that human beings live together, Brecht provides us with unique inspiration.

It's striking just how unshakeable was Brecht's own dedication to this double objective. In 1939, as Hitler's armies were massing for their rampage across Europe, he asked:

> How can the theatre be both instructive and
> entertaining? How can it be divorced from spiritual dope
> traffic and turned from a home of illusions to a home of
> experience? How can the unfree, ignorant man of our
> century, with his thirst for freedom and his hunger for
> knowledge; how can the tortured and heroic, abused and
> ingenious, changeable and world-changing man of this
> great and ghastly century obtain his own theatre which
> will help him to master the world and himself?[1]

In one of the darkest years of the century, Brecht was clinging on heroically to the hope of a theatre that could make a difference.

Many people have tried to take up Brecht's challenge: the German political theatre of the 1960s, the collectivism of Dario Fo and Franca Rame, the work of Giorgio Strehler at the Piccolo Theatre in Milan, the agitprop of the San Francisco Mime Troupe, the populism of Joan Littlewood's Theatre Workshop in London, the aestheticism of George Devine's Royal Court, the forum theatre of Augusto Boal, the colourful internationalism of Ariane Mnouchkine's Théâtre du Soleil and the magisterial productions of Peter Stein at the Schaubühne in Berlin and elsewhere. Dozens of smaller companies in the 1970s brought a more immediate kind of Brechtianism to their work: 7:84, Belt and Braces, Red Ladder, Joint Stock and many others.

Brecht occupies a strange position today. His influence is visible everywhere, from the most politically explicit theatre to performance art, from new plays to revivals of the classics, from art house to community theatre. But his own theatre is frequently thought to be cold, lacking in human feeling and politically irrelevant. What's more, the productions of his plays that are most critically admired are usually ones that travesty his intentions.

Thankfully, our experience cannot compare with the horrors that Brecht faced in the 1930s and '40s, and few of us have a tenth of his political and artistic commitment. But we live in strange times and, for all the freedoms that we enjoy, our political options are narrowly circumscribed. In an age in which the consumer is king, political parties formulate policy through focus groups, and are only successful when they occupy the centre ground. We're expected to accept certain assumptions about the way that society should be run: imposing higher taxation on the rich is dismissed as counterproductive, trade unionists are mocked as dinosaurs, and economic liberalism is hailed as the only show in town. Developing an argument – let alone a kind of theatre – which can challenge these glib assumptions is difficult, some would say impossible. But Brecht would insist that we have no choice but to try. And that's the nature of his challenge to those of us 'born later'.

ONE DIRECTOR'S EXPERIENCE

No one has influenced my work as a director as much as Brecht. I've only worked on two of his plays, but his approach is inscribed deep in my directorial DNA. What follows is an account of how it has shaped five very different productions over the last twenty-five years.

The Decision

In 1987 I was invited to direct Brecht's controversial *Lehrstück The Decision* (*Die Maßnahme*, usually translated as *The Measures Taken*) at the Almeida Music Festival.

Concerned that it would be misunderstood, Brecht forbade all professional performances.[2] In 1987, however, John Willett managed to persuade the two heirs – Stefan Brecht and George Eisler – that the time had come to present it as an artefact from a very different world. So he wrote a new translation,[3] with songs and choruses that fitted Hanns Eisler's original music, and dialogue with an energy and accuracy that the existing one lacked. This was a historic occasion: the first time Brecht's most explosive play had been presented in its entirety since 1930.

The Decision takes the form of a report by four Communist party members who have just returned from a cross-border operation into Imperial China, agitating for the Revolution. They report the death of one of their comrades and enact a series of episodes which show what led up to his death: his emotional empathy for the poor and the oppressed endangered the overall operation and he was eventually – and with his agreement – shot and his body was thrown into a lime pit. The Party express their agreement with their 'decision'. Understandably, it's controversial stuff.[4]

The Decision has been much criticised – above all for its apparent justification of Stalin's purges – and so it was essential that we understood something of the historical context. We remembered that the international Communist movement of the

1930s – like the early Christians, or the Jihadis today – saw martyrdom and sacrifice as necessary to the struggle. We acknowledged the real-life experiences of Eisler's brother, Gerhart, and sister, Ruth Fischer, both of whom had been involved in agitation in China, and understood that many of Brecht's friends and colleagues had worked for the Party in Germany and elsewhere. Finally, we recalled that, in 1930, Hitler was on the verge of seizing power and violence between Nazi thugs and Communist cadres was a daily occurrence in the streets of Berlin. The dangers involved in fighting for a better world were all too real to Brecht, Eisler and their collaborators, and without such historical context, the piece would be meaningless.

The Decision's dramatic form is challenging. It requires three actors and a tenor, and a large choir. The score demands a small band – all brass and percussion – and a piano. It consists of a series of eight short dramatic scenes, sometimes with individual musical numbers, punctuated by a series of large-scale chorales. The overall effect is reminiscent of a Bach mass: a familiar and exceptionally powerful dramatic story is told simply and powerfully, and the chorales expand and meditate on the issues raised.

The Decision was written as a learning piece for the original participants. Our production was performed at the Union Chapel in Islington with a large – and entirely apolitical[5] – choir. We placed them and the band over the altar, and built a small white platform stage across the first three or four rows of pews. The four actors sat on four chairs, which they brought forward when required. Each episode was staged with the minimum of fuss, simply and directly, with a handful of props being cleared the moment the protagonists returned to direct reporting. A rope was held across the stage for the 'Song of the Rice-Barge Hauliers', a simple bowl of rice was used for the dinner that the Merchant offers the Young Comrade, a bright-red pamphlet was torn up by the Young Comrade when he turns his back on the 'Classics' (of Communism), and the escape was dramatised by a simple running on the spot. Nothing appeared on the small white stage that wasn't used directly in the action.

There were two contentious points. The first was Brecht's insistence that each of the four performers should take it in turns to play the Young Comrade. Brecht was worried that the audience would personalise the issues and see them as a product of 'character' rather than 'tactics'. But I decided that the audience needed the sense of an individual – the piece is, after all, about the limitations of the individual in a communal effort – and the fresh-faced Adam Robertson played the part throughout. I think I was right to do this but I know that the true Brechtian would have disagreed.

The other contentious point was John Willett's insistence that all the verse should be addressed directly to the audience. In rehearsal we found this difficult: it seemed overly artificial and uncomfortable. But John was right: with direct address, the piece took on the character of a public debate and – as in Greek tragedy and in Shakespeare – the awareness of the audience brought out the intricacies of the political discussion.

We performed *The Decision* the night of the 1987 General Election, when Mrs Thatcher achieved her third election triumph – hardly a ringing endorsement of the impact of political theatre! The great and the good of the British left turned out to see this extraordinary relic of their youth given its due. We received many compliments but our approach was utterly pragmatic.[6] We had a very good cast – Stephen Dillane, Tilda Swinton, Adam Robertson[7] and the tenor Philip Doghan – and we rehearsed it very carefully. We never forgot that the drama consists of a 'report' and we ensured that everything had the right demonstrative feel. We enjoyed Brecht's theatrical innovations but never discussed his theory. Above all, we found ourselves in awe at the scale of Brecht and Eisler's artistic achievement and were constantly amazed – and sometimes shocked – by the directness of its central message: 'Change the world. It needs it.'

Man to Man

In 1987 I directed the British premiere of Manfred Karge's one-woman play, *Man to Man* (*Jacke Wie Hose*),[8] at the Traverse Theatre in Edinburgh, and then at the Royal Court.

Manfred Karge (born 1938) started his career as an actor at the Berliner Ensemble. Although he never met Brecht, his work as actor, director and writer was dominated by his influence. Indeed, some claim that Karge, along with the writer Heiner Müller and the director Matthias Langhoff, are among Brecht's most important German disciples. He still directs at the Berliner Ensemble.

Man to Man is a remarkable monologue. Written in twenty-six short episodes – some in prose, some verse, interspersed with quotations from popular culture, fragments of songs, and so on – the piece tells the story of Ella Gericke, a woman who survived the depression, the Nazis, and the division of Germany, by disguising herself as her dead husband, Max, and taking over his job as a crane driver. It's the story of a divided person and a bitterly divided country.

Alienation is both the subject of *Man to Man* and its technique. It shows how, in a world gone mad, a woman is alienated from her own nature, and has to become someone else in order to survive; it demonstrates how her deepest instincts are obscured, destroyed even, by the social forces at work on her; and it dramatises the way that even her language is distorted by the battery of lies, clichés, slogans and nonsense that have invaded her loneliness. And this social alienation is expressed in the play's theatrical style, with its fractured text, episodic jump-cuts, epic time frame and multiple perspectives. The Marxist and the Brechtian notions of alienation have rarely been so brilliantly fused.

The play has no stage directions and hardly any punctuation. The scenes give no indication of location and the text reads like a collection of poems and fragments, each with its own number, style and impact. Karge directed the play's premiere and its deliberately blank presentation is a reflection of that. But it's also a piece of alienation in its own right: in other words, anybody wanting to perform the play has to make a series of conscious and creative decisions – interventions, if you like – as to how it should be staged.

I took a risk in casting the young Tilda Swinton (she was twenty-seven) as Ella/Max Gericke. The play is told from the perspective of an old, working-class woman, looking back on her life: this young, aristocratic, Cambridge-educated beauty was hardly appropriate casting. But it also requires the most forceful commitment to a kind of acting which is highly alienated, informed by intelligence, analysis and wit. Tilda, needless to say, was magnificent.

The first challenge – once we'd understood the point of each of the scenes – which the designer Bunny Christie, Tilda and I faced was to come up with a wide range of theatrical styles that could reflect their unique characteristics. We then needed to find a frame in which these wildly contradictory elements could be presented. We settled on a simple white box, littered with 'junky' objects: a fridge (with a horrible yellow light in it), a group of miniature Christmas trees, a rabbit in a cage, a cheap amplifier and a microphone on a stand, a variety of chairs, a tinny tape recorder, and a red-tape line down the middle of the floor. The result was a postmodern collage.

To express something of the character's alienation, Tilda wore crusty white make-up throughout (with yellow cigarette-stained teeth and fingers), a short shock wig, heavy black boots, a sleeveless man's vest and coloured Y-fronts. We also scattered a series of costume suggestions around the stage: a woolly hat, a pink housecoat, an all-in-one jacket, shirt and tie, a ballet tutu, and so on, which she donned occasionally to illustrate a scene. We dealt with the all-important question of gender in the most literal, brutal fashion: her breasts were wrapped in cling film, and she stuck a pair of socks down her Y-fronts as a cock.[9]

We looked for deliberate stylistic discontinuities. Indeed, we agreed that every 'number' required its own distinct theatrical style, and that such stylistic contradictions would bring out the contradictions in the text – and in the character. And so one was played as Stanislavskian naturalism, the next as stand-up comedy, one had the feel of music-hall patter, another was mock-Shakespearean rhetoric; sometimes the text was presented as a series of tongue-twisters, at other times as a piece of pop-up, disposable, poor theatre – for example, Tilda spraying red ketchup across the white wall to suggest the spilt blood of the Nazi years, and drawing with a marker pen a small prison cell to describe the time when Max was arrested.

The production was a critical and popular success, and later made into a film. The overwhelming impression was of one woman's desperate struggle for survival in a world gone mad. That struggle required a profound personal alienation and the play's radical theatrical style caught that alienation perfectly.

Don Giovanni

Mozart's *Don Giovanni* is perhaps the most dramatic of all operas, and many distinguished directors have been defeated by its considerable challenges. So when Garsington Opera asked me to stage it in 2002, I was terrified.

The traditional romantic reading of *Don Giovanni* is of a charming rogue who eventually gets his comeuppance. Modern directors tend either to emphasise the opera's cynicism (Giovanni gets away with murder and is given the best tunes) or to interpret it in a post-Freudian fashion, as a study in dominance and submission in sexual relationships. I was unconvinced by both.

I was struck, however, by the detail of Da Ponte's remarkable libretto, which combines a tremendous celebration of the central character's rebellious ego with a profound questioning of the cost paid by others to sustain it. It struck me that Giovanni is *both* a radical – a rebel against God, father and society – *and* a dangerous, reactionary predator, and that this combination lies at the heart of the opera's power. I then came across Brecht's description of Molière's Dom Juan as an 'aristocratic tiger'[10] and tried to work out the value of this fascinating contradiction in practice.

I knew that I could only make sense of the piece if I presented it within a coherent social context. I knew that it isn't enough to see the Don just as a seducer; he needs to be seen as an *aristocratic* seducer. Likewise, it's essential that Donna Anna is as aristocratic as the Don, a woman whose sexual identity is tied up with her position in society (as expressed in her betrothal to the noble Don Ottavio and her relationship with her father the Commendatore). And I also felt that Donna Elvira needed to be seen as more of a 'bourgeois' than Anna, so that her abandonment by Giovanni is more of an emotional hurt than a social humiliation. And, finally, I realised that Giovanni's attempted seduction of Zerlina – and subsequent confrontation with Masetto – embodies in the most physical form the social exploitation of the peasantry by the aristocracy.

The mistake is to imagine that the characters relate to each other in simple psychological terms, and grasping this complex network of class relations is crucial. I realised that if we managed to 'alienate' the title role, and not see him as the only subject of the opera, we'd gain a huge amount: above all, the audience would understand that an aristocrat like this, raping and plundering his way through society, needs to be opposed; what's more, we'd understand that Masetto, Ottavio and the Commendatore are not necessarily the moralistic cardboard cutouts of the modern tradition.

The danger, of course, with all of this social realism – which is borne out by the astonishing libretto and (dare I say it?) by the music – is that we lose sight of the lush sensuality of the opera. But Brecht's embrace of the pleasurable helped me see that it was possible to forge a dramatic style that celebrated the opera's physicality while also showing us its vivid social, psychological and political realism.

The more I worked on *Don Giovanni*, the more I came to notice its epic structure. The story is told through a series of episodes, each with a very contrasting tone, a perfect example of Brecht's 'epic theatre'. And a production benefits from embodying these shifting locations, times and style. The mistake, as Brecht would have pointed out, is to smooth the edges, or try to iron out the contradictions.

Jackie Brooks's design consisted of a beautifully proportioned, stained wooden box, with hidden doors set into the walls. She suggested locations by occasional pieces of furniture, and the raising and lowering of a long bench that emerged from the floor. Other visual interpretation was kept to a minimum, with the dramatic action unfolding through carefully costumed figures set in striking and continually moving tableaux.

I knew that Giovanni's final descent into Hell deserved something special, if only a kind of theatricality that acknowledged the end as a conventional deus ex machina – after all, few people today believe in any afterlife at all, let alone the torments of Hell. But it's not good enough to see it *simply* metaphorically: and so in our production the floorboards slid open, red-paper flames appeared (blown by hidden fans), and Giovanni was dragged inexorably into the gap. After that, of course, the floorboards rejoined each other, the flames disappeared, and the righteous celebrated the downfall of their enemy.

Don Giovanni is one of the great masterpieces of eighteenth-century theatre. It's hardly surprising that Brecht, with his careful study of the revolutionary drama of the European bourgeoisie, offers a model of a kind of theatre that is tremendously liberating when we come to stage one of these great works. It was interesting to see how many people felt that this 'Brechtian' production brought out so much that was latent in the piece.

King Lear

I first read *King Lear* when I was fourteen, and I was thrilled when the opportunity finally arose to direct the play for my company English Touring Theatre (ETT) in 2002. I assembled a strong cast, led by Timothy West, and we toured the country, bringing it to the Old Vic in Spring 2003.

In preparation I revisited Jan Kott's '*King Lear* or *Endgame*'[11] (which I'd last read as an eighteen-year-old!); I watched Grigori Kozintsev's extraordinary film of the play (1971) and went back to Wilson Knight's essay '*King Lear* and the Comedy of the Grotesque'.[12] I also reread Margot Heinemann's brilliant '*King Lear* and the World Turned Upside Down'.[13]

In their different ways, these shaped my thinking. Jan Kott draws a parallel between *Lear* and the theatre of the absurd – especially Beckett's *Endgame* – and the essay was especially influential on Peter Brook, whose famous RSC production in 1962 has done a huge amount to shape the modern tradition. But I recognised that, while Kott illuminates some passages (e.g. 'As flies to wanton boys are we to the gods, / They kill us for their sport'), it was not enough to see the play in such a narrow and existential fashion. Some of the characters reach a point of despair in which the world seems to have no meaning, but that isn't true of the whole society. Stimulating as Kott is, it's not enough.

Kozintsev's great film of the play (and his book *The Space of Tragedy*) reminded me that, although *King Lear* focuses on the interlinked stories of two powerful families, the entire society is caught up in the consequences of their actions. This contrasts with Wilson Knight, who helped dislodge residual, Bradley-esque notions of regal nobility, but fails to give the play a broader social context.

It struck me forcefully that Lear's vanity and use of arbitrary power is the catalyst for the chaos that engulfs him. As is Gloucester's gullibility and superstition. Crucially, however, I realised that the social changes that the play enacts are not all negative. Or rather – and here Brecht's reading of Shakespeare, especially *The Messingkauf Dialogues*, helped – I wanted to show the contradictory forces at work, and do everything I could to point out that the final outcome is not inevitable. A series of individual decisions are made which leads to the catastrophe.

I was eager to give a clear sense of the descent from order into chaos: Margot Heinemann's essay reminded me that Lear's

Albion isn't a dysfunctional dictatorship, as is sometimes played, and that the King isn't 'mad at the beginning'. The first scene shows a King whose plans for political succession are driven by an excess of personal emotion and insufficient political savoir-faire. But the important thing is that there must be somewhere to go.

King Lear was written in the dark years following James I's accession in 1603, and reflects the social fragmentation and growing conflict that was leading inexorably to the Civil War. I was eager to dramatise the social forces that brought about the gradual degeneration of the society, 'the world turned upside down'. I was struck by the attention Shakespeare pays to the poor and the excluded, and was fascinated by the realistic detail with which he draws these 'minor characters'. I was especially interested in the critical episodes which trigger the changes in the social order: the first servant who kills Cornwall and so changes the course of history; the blind Gloucester giving his purse to a poor man and declaring that 'distribution shall undo excess / And each man have enough'; and the mad King praying to the 'poor naked wretches' who he and his like have ignored.

Somehow – with a small budget and only fourteen actors – I had to find expression for the social dynamics that the play dramatises so brilliantly. I prepared a new, very lightly punctuated, and carefully cut edition of the text.[14] Our physical production had a striking simplicity, which paid homage to Caspar Neher and the Berliner Ensemble. The designer Neil Warmington came up with a simple raised wooden platform (made of old timber) surrounded by a simple white cyclorama. A section of the floor lifted up to create a hovel, and a number of large framed photographs of the Moon and the Earth were suspended from time to time to suggest the cosmic scale of the piece. Otherwise the entire action of the play was told through an ever-changing series of simple but striking groupings of figures wearing carefully designed and detailed costumes from the 1640s.

I regard this production as one of the best things I've ever directed. It's also the most Brechtian. When it comes to the great political plays of Shakespeare, Brecht's epic realism is, I believe, the finest theatrical model we have.

The Winslow Boy

2011 saw the centenary of Terence Rattigan's birth. In 2009 (two years too early, perhaps) I directed a major revival of one of his finest plays, *The Winslow Boy* (1946). Sometimes dismissed as a 'rep warhorse', it's an astonishingly fine piece about family and the enduring importance of justice: 'Let Right be Done!' is a phrase that echoes down through the generations and, in the light of the ongoing debate about the rights of suspected terrorists and other 'a-socials', seemed extraordinarily pertinent, as did the jokes and questions about the integrity of Parliament set against the furore over Members' expenses at the time.

As usual, I found it important to see the play within its historical context. Although written in the aftermath of the Second World War, the action is set on the eve of the First World War. It's striking that, in writing about the core principles of justice and human rights, Rattigan should have turned from his own time – with the grotesque crimes of the Nazis fresh in everybody's mind – to an apparently more innocent time. But Rattigan's purpose was more sophisticated and he brilliantly dramatised the last moment of idealism, in a world increasingly threatened by warmongering. If a boy such as Ronnie Winslow can be wrongly convicted of the theft of a 'bally ten-bob postal order', then what exactly are we fighting for?

I knew that it was important to be clear about the Winslows. It's all too easy to assume that they are a conventional Edwardian family. But Rattigan's conception is more interesting and is deliberately based on contradiction. Arthur Winslow is a very particular kind of patriarch: he expects his children to be truthful, intelligent and independent-minded. He is exasperated by his son Dickie's light-headedness and has far more time for his daughter Kate, a suffragette and a radical. And he believes in his youngest son Ronnie's protestations of his innocence.

The actress playing Kate had to be particularly careful of the contradictions implicit in her character. It was essential that the audience got the measure of her radicalism and did not patronise her. But it was also important to acknowledge the importance to a young woman in her mid-twenties in that time to be married. I knew that Kate had to be genuinely affected by her fiancé John, and upset by his breaking off their engagement; but I also insisted that the audience could only understand the nature of her sacrifice if they came to appreciate the solid appeal of *his* conventionality.

I recognised that the presentation of the barrister Sir Robert Morton posed another challenge. Not only is he astonishingly arrogant and effortlessly upper-class, he's also a Tory. But Brecht would have reminded us not only that class is an aggregation of frequently contradictory attitudes, but also that the struggle for justice and human rights can appear in the most unlikely of figures. The surprising thing is the way that the victims of injustice so frequently do nothing to remedy the situation. Brecht's demand for 'complex seeing' couldn't be more apposite.

'Let Right be Done' is strikingly resonant in *The Winslow Boy* and is still of fundamental importance in any discussion of the meaning of justice. Brecht, I think, would have approved, even if he would have been surprised to discover writing of genuine political insight and radical inspiration coming from one of the most consummately commercial of upper-middle-class English playwrights.

CONCLUSION

Brecht's impact on the modern British theatre has been huge, but his plays are often seen as doctrinaire and dull, and his theories dismissed as incomprehensible. Defending Brecht is a lonely business.

In 1934, a year after Hitler's coming to power, Brecht wrote one of his clearest and most beautifully expressed statements about his approach to the theatre:

> Such is our time, and the theatre must be acquainted with it and go along with it, and work out an entirely new sort of art such as will be capable of influencing modern people. The main subject of the drama must be relationships between one man and another as they exist today, and that is what I'm primarily concerned to investigate and find means of expression for. Once I've found what modes of behaviour are most useful to the human race I show them to people and underline them. I show them in parables: if you act this way the following will happen, but if you act like that then the opposite will take place.[15]

It combines a sense of the dark times in which he is living, with a plea for a kind of theatre which could stand as a counterweight to the barbarism that had engulfed his homeland and was about to sweep across Europe. It's as good a way as any to end this necessarily sketchy introduction to Brecht and his unique approach to theatre.

In a time of increasing economic disorder, social upheaval and political instability, the theatre should engage with the world outside the stage door. And Brecht's unique mixture of radical innovation and classical restraint, scepticism and hope, deep seriousness and anarchic wit, points the way.

1. 'On Experimental Theatre' (1939).
2. For an account of Brecht's prohibition on performances of *The Decision*, see John Willett's notes in Volume 3ii of *The Collected Works*.
3. Published in Volume 3ii of *The Collected Works*.
4. A few years later the Austrian novelist Stefan Zweig wrote his masterpiece *Beware of Pity* (1938): its title could be used to describe *The Decision*.
5. A left-wing friend of mine especially enjoyed seeing the choir – an amateur choir made up of headmasters, bankers, stockbrokers, etc. – belting out 'we are the scum of the earth'.
6. See John Willett's 'Ups and Downs of British Brecht' in *Reinterpreting Brecht* (1990).
7. Tragically, this talented young actor died in a motorcycle accident in 1988.
8. Manfred Karge's *Man to Man* and *The Conquest of the South Pole* were published together in translations by Tinch Minter and Anthony Vivis (1988).
9. Tilda and I had many conversations about what it feels like to be a man: I remember her whoop of joy when she first put the socks down her Y-fronts.
10. Notes to Brecht's adapation of *Dom Juan* in *Collected Plays, Vol 9* (US only, 1972).
11. Jan Kott, *Shakespeare our Contemporary* (1964).
12. G. Wilson Knight, *The Wheel of Fire* (1930).
13. Margot Heinemann, 'Demystifying the state: *King Lear* and the World Turned Upside Down', in *Shakespeare and Politics* (1992).
14. Published by Oberon Books (2002).
15. 'Interview with an Exile' (1934).

5

Exercises

5

Exercises

TWO CONFESSIONS

Let me preface this chapter with two confessions. The first is my own. I am one of the most Brechtian of British theatre directors. I see plays in social and political terms; I want to create a theatre rich with observations into how people live with each other, and how history unfolds; I am eager to approach plays – and life – in an inquisitive and challenging way; and I use many of the trademarks of the Brechtian theatre in my practice. But the honest truth is I never, ever, ask actors to do exercises which will help them 'act with alienation', or understand 'the epic theatre', or show up the 'contradictions' in their character. I don't think I've ever spoken about 'gestus' in rehearsals, or consciously pursued any of the other Brechtian techniques. And so, in writing this book, which is intended as an introduction to Brecht's theatrical practice, I was stumped when I realised that it needed to include some practical exercises if it was to be of use to students. My Brechtianism is so fundamental to the way that I work that I didn't know what to suggest.

I was thrilled, therefore, to meet Julian Jones, Senior Lecturer in Acting at Rose Bruford College of Theatre and Performance, and delighted when he offered to create a series of exercises which could help young actors and others understand the fundamentals of Brechtian acting. (He too has a confession to make, as you'll soon see.)

Julian worked with a group of remarkable young people (see my acknowledgements earlier) in a spirit of fun and adventure to

create the exercises that follow. They are not designed as Brechtian 'holy writ'; instead, they are to be adapted, questioned,
challenged and, if necessary, rejected. But, most importantly,
they are to be enjoyed: 'Nothing needs less justification than
pleasure,' as Brecht memorably put it.

First, though, Julian's personal account of his own journey –
what we might call 'the confessions of a non-Brechtian':

As an actor I never really got Brecht, and in twenty-odd years of
acting in television and theatre I never once consulted his
theoretical works. Conversely, when I was introduced to
Stanislavsky at RADA, it was a revelation. A second epiphany
came later when I discovered Sanford Meisner. Both
Stanislavsky and Meisner were actors as well as teachers, and
the systems they developed grew directly out of their experience
as actors in response to the practical problems they faced. These
were systems conceived, developed and honed by actors for
actors – practical, do-able and (for the most part) simple.

Brecht, on the other hand, was a writer and director and his
ideas, as expressed in his theoretical writings, were, I thought,
best suited to the academy and were of no real practical use to
the actor. However, when I became a teacher at Rose Bruford I
was forced to reconsider Brechtian theory, woven as it was into
the training, where it forms a central part of the curriculum.
That was six years ago and I am still grappling with these ideas
– I particularly struggle when I am thinking predominantly as
an actor.

Over the past six years, however, the clouds have gradually
begun to lift. This is in part due to an ongoing debate with my
colleague David Zoob. Our sparring – Brechtian director versus
Stanislavskian actor – comes to a head every year when we
deliver a workshop on Brecht to MA Directing students at
Birkbeck College. I say 'we'; actually David delivers the
workshop using me as his guinea pig. And it's during these
sessions that I am forced to grapple with Brechtian ideas, not in
theory but in practice, as an actor – on my own, vulnerable,
exposed (as actors are) in a room full of scrutinising directors –

trying to communicate the intrinsic meaning of scenes from plays not only by Brecht but also by Chekhov and Sophocles. At the end of the session my head hurts, and I often feel that I have not acted in the 'right way', that is in an appropriately 'Brechtian style'. Frankly, this is because I am uncertain what a 'Brechtian style of acting' is. When I analyse the experience after the event and try to pinpoint what the problem is, I come back to the same few observations:

- I don't know where my head is – that is, I don't know where to place my attention (contrary to the Stanislavskian approach where one's attention is on one's objective or, as Meisner insists, on the other actors).

- I am confused by the attempt to fully play more than one thing at a time (see Meisner's assertion that this is not possible).

- I struggle with the Brechtian notion of 'commenting' on the character that I am playing.

- I can't get to grips with the idea that one can play the politics or social context of a scene – surely as an actor you just enter imaginatively into the given circumstances of the world of the play and pursue your character's objective through the playing of actions, adapting responsively and in the moment to the behaviour and actions of the other actors and the surrounding environment?

To be fair, I have, over these six years, increasingly understood Brechtian theory and its undeniable contribution to the disciplines of dramaturgy, direction and the staging of plays. Its significance for those who passionately believe that theatre can and should function in society as something more than just 'entertainment' has also become clear. Consequently, Brechtian ideas have increasingly influenced my practice as a teacher and director.

The real sticking point for me is when I am working as an actor. I find myself returning to the same fundamental question, which goes something like this: 'Okay, I get the ideas, I see their application for the director and the playwright, particularly in relation to dramaturgy. I think I understand what you, the director, are asking me, the actor, to show... But... what I can't get my head round is: HOW do I do it?!?! With Stanislavsky I pursue an objective, I play an action, I use 'the magic if', etc. With Meisner I 'work off' the other actors spontaneously, on impulse, in the present moment. What do I, the actor, do to put into practice these Brechtian ideas? How do I act? The following exercises have been developed in an attempt to answer these questions from the perspective of the actor – they are practical, and should be simple, clear and enjoyable.

That, at least, is the hope!

THE ENSEMBLE

Developing an epic sensibility

1: Lying and Leaping

Purpose

▸ To warm up and to bring everyone's attention into the room.
▸ To establish a sense of the group or the collective.
▸ To heighten awareness and to place your attention outside of yourself and on the group as a whole.
▸ To develop a sense of trust and fun within the ensemble.

Description

Everyone walks around the space freely and with energy. Everyone places their attention outside of themselves and on the group as a whole – looking each other in the eyes. Notice where your attention is – if it is on yourself, then let that go, and place it on the other members of the ensemble. Allow yourselves as a group to find the moment when, collectively, you all lie down on the floor. Everyone then gets back up and continues to walk around the room as before. Repeat this sequence two or three times.

Stage two is the same only, this time, rather than lying down, everyone, together, leaps into the air with a cry of joy. Repeat stage two a couple of times. The aim is that no one leads the lying and leaping – rather, by developing a sense of trust and fun within the ensemble, you all act together. This exercise is not as easy as it sounds – but as the group develops a sense of trust and ease it is remarkable how quickly the ability to work together in this way evolves. Eventually, the effect should be that the group moves together like a flock of birds or a shoal of fish.

2: Tuning In

Purpose

▸ To establish a sense of the group/ensemble.
▸ To sharpen powers of observation.
▸ To develop the ability to copy accurately what you observe.

Description

The group forms a circle (as wide as possible). Everyone then copies/mirrors what is happening in the whole group – both what they *see* and what they *hear*. It is important that no one 'leads' this. Each individual acts in response to the group as a whole. Your attention is outside of yourself and on the other members of the group – you are following, not leading.

3: The Person Through the Walk

Purpose

▸ To introduce the concept of 'alienation' in a way that involves the group as a whole. Observation is the key. This is an initial 'way in' to physical characterisation.

Description 3.1

One person walks around the space. It helps if the walker has a 'daydream' – this makes them less self-conscious and prevents them from listening to the comments of the workshop leader. The rest of the group observe the walker intently, while considering the following questions:

- Where do they lead from? Forehead, chin, nose, chest, groin, knees, etc.?
- What is their tempo-rhythm? Do they move from side to side, or directly forward? Do they sway or are they stiff?
- What element might they be? Are they earthed or light? Do they glide, or stomp?
- What do their arms do?
- Where are they tense or loose?

After a minute or so of this, another member of the group joins the walker, walking just behind them and mimicking their walk as accurately as possible in all respects. After thirty seconds or so, another group member joins, mimicking the person directly in front of them. Continue this process until the whole group is walking in the space in a chain. The original walker then stops leading and joins the end of the line, mimicking the person directly in front of them. After a few seconds, the rest of the group sit down and re-observe the original walker.

The question is: how close to the original walk is the final walk? The original walker may discover something about their habitual walk that they were not previously aware of – they see and experience their familiar walk in a new and unfamiliar way.

Description 3.2

In another version, each walker exaggerates slightly at least one characteristic of the walker in front of them. When the original walker comes to take over they are adopting an estranged version of their original walk – they are made aware of the way in which they walk and are in a position to ask the question: 'What aspects of my walk, if any, are a result of my social being'?

4: Grandmother's Footsteps*

Purpose

▶ Introducing the concept of 'gestus'.
▶ To construct living, active and (in 4.3 and 4.4) socially engaged stage pictures or tableaux.
▶ To develop a physically engaged and connected ensemble or chorus.
▶ To increase (in 4.3 and 4.4) a sense of social and political awareness within the ensemble as an engaged collective, particularly in relation to contemporary social issues.
▶ This warm-up exercise is particularly useful for actors working on crowd scenes or Chorus (the Chorus of Elders in Brecht's *Antigone*, for instance).

Description 4.1

Start a game of 'Grandmother's Footsteps'. This can involve either the whole group or a portion of the group while the others observe. Notice the vitality, focus and 'togetherness' of the 'group pictures' that are created at the moment when the person who is trying to catch them out turns round.

Description 4.2

The same, but this time with obstacles. These obstacles (chairs or tables, for example) the group has to negotiate (crawl under, climb over, etc.) on their journey to the 'turner'.

Description 4.3

The same only, this time, add socially specific circumstances and give the group a socially charged identity. For instance, the social situation could be the London riots. The 'turner'

---

*   This exercise, in its original form, was introduced to Julian Jones by his Rose Bruford colleague, David Zoob.

could be a policeman or, alternatively, a shopkeeper guarding their shop. The crowd could be the rioters. Alternatively, the 'turner' could be a rioter and the crowd could be the police, etc.

Description 4.4

The same, but now give each individual member of the crowd a specific socially grounded identity, and perhaps a particular task. For instance, a single mother with a baby – the task being to protect the baby while at the same time trying to steal some baby clothes from a shop. Observers should note the sharp focus and vitality of the socially charged stage pictures that are formed when the group freezes.

5: Seeing Afresh

Purpose

▸ Again, a way of introducing the concepts of 'alienation' and 'gestus' through collective play and the creation of *tableaux vivants*. This exercise is especially useful when working on a scene where a group or crowd of people (with either a common or diverse socially determined perspective) have to be in relation to a particular object. The various members of the Florentine Court, for instance, when contemplating Galileo's telescope. Or the group of early-morning shoppers who suddenly notice the hanging body of the butcher in his shop window in 'The Old Militant' scene (*Fear and Misery of the Third Reich*).

Description 5.1

The whole group walk around the room. They pay attention to the environment. After a minute or so they allow themselves to notice something in the room *as if* (to use the

Stanislavskian phrase) for the first time. This could be large
or small – on the ceiling, wall or floor – an object or simply a
mark. When something has caught their attention, they stop
still and focus their attention on that thing – they may stand,
crouch, kneel, lie, etc., while they contemplate the object or
mark. Others in the group who are still moving in the space
can join someone who has stopped and join in the
contemplation of the object/mark.

Small groups of 'observers' may form. Only the original
'observer' who first noticed the object/mark can break the
contemplation by moving away – this releases the group to
carry on moving through the space. Each individual keeps
moving through the space until they either notice something
themselves or join another 'observer' who has stopped to
contemplate something. The object or mark of attention
takes on a defamiliarised (alienated) aspect.

Description 5.2

The same, only this time the 'observer' and those joining
reach out to the object or mark – they do this with an
attitude to the it (e.g. with love, trepidation, awe, disgust,
etc.). Everyone may adopt different physical positions in
relation to the object or mark and to each other, and may all
reach out to it in different ways. Again, 'living pictures' that
portray particular attitudes are created in the space.

Description 5.3

The same, but with various socially specific given
circumstances being dictated by the workshop leader. For
example (to continue with the 'London riots' scenario): the
scene could be the residents of Hackney coming out onto
the streets to survey the damage done to their
neighbourhood on the morning following the night of the
riots, or New Yorkers coming out onto the streets of their
city on the morning following 9/11.

6: *Have You Been Looking?*

Purpose

▶ To remind the ensemble of the importance of observation.

▶ To continue to establish a sense of fun and further draw the group towards becoming an ensemble.

Description

The group again forms a wide circle, filling the space, and the workshop leader asks them to turn outwards, making sure that they can't see each other. The workshop leader then asks individuals to describe other individuals in the circle as fully and accurately as possible – What are they wearing, what is their hair like? Sleeves rolled up or down, shoes on or off, any jewellery?, etc.

This exercise requires the group to at least know each other by name. By now a sense of the ensemble should be beginning to take hold of the group, as well as a readiness to experiment freely with a sense of fun.

STORY AND NARRATIVE

Communicating the story with clarity and precision:
what must we show?

For most of the exercises that follow it's best to work with
duologues – plays that have an explicit social or political
dimension are especially useful (David Mamet's Oleanna,
Howard Barker's The Possibilities, *several of the scenes from*
Fear and Misery of the Third Reich, *and The Prologue from*
Brecht's adaptation of Antigone *are good examples).*

7: Show and Tell

Purpose

▶ To clarify, both for the actors playing the scene
  and for the rest of the ensemble watching, what
  the story is – particularly in relation to the
  socio-political world of the play and its
  characters.

Description

Take a chunk of text, perhaps two pages of dialogue
(preferably a duologue). Unit the text, identifying the
narrative shifts. The actors then play the scene, a unit at a
time. Firstly, they act the scene in the 'usual' way – in other
words, they dramatise the narrative, they show us the story.
They then immediately go back to the beginning of the unit
and this time they *tell* us the story; they narrate it to us (the
rest of the ensemble). They do this in the third person and in
the past tense. This event then becomes something that
happened in the past. When narrating the story, the actors

may have an attitude to that story – this could be the attitude of the actor or character (perhaps try first one then the other).

This attitude may be that of a 'knowing amusement', for instance – we in the audience are made to see the 'funny side' of the event. The actors then show the next unit, then narrate that unit – and so on. The other members of the ensemble may suggest ways in which either the dramatisation or the narration could be played in order to make the story clearer. This is informed by and informs the company's understanding of what the story is about; what it means – particularly in relation to its socio-political context. The group could use this exercise as a way of exploring the socio-political dynamics that operate between 'The Man' and 'The Wife' in 'The Spy' (Scene Ten of *Fear and Misery of the Third Reich*).

8: This is What Happened

Purpose

▶ To clarify, both for the actors playing the scene and the rest of the ensemble watching, what the story is by focusing on the key events – this time from the point of view of the observer. This exercise may be particularly useful for an actor who is working on a narrator figure – Alfieri in Arthur Miller's *A View from the Bridge*, or Wang in *The Good Person of Szechwan*, for instance.

Description

As in the previous exercise, the actors act, dramatise or show us a unit of action, or perhaps the whole chunk of selected dialogue (about two pages of text). This time it is one of the observing ensemble members that then gets up and narrates the story (again in the third person and in the past tense – again with an attitude). They may demonstrate physically and vocally how the characters in the story behaved, how they did what they did and said what they said (see Brecht's essay 'The Street Scene'). A second ensemble member may ask the narrator for clarification at any point in order to enhance the precision, simplicity and economy of the storytelling.

9: What's Yer Pitch, Kid?

Purpose

▸ To develop in the actor the ability to isolate the key points of a story and do so with precision, economy and clarity.

Description

Each member of the ensemble takes it in turn to make a 'pitch' to either the whole group or a selected 'producer' or team of producers. This should be done 'in character' – give the 'pitcher' (who could be writer, director, actor, etc.) a character (perhaps with a political agenda or bias) and set of given circumstances – plus a reason to pitch a play, film, TV series, and an attitude to this particular project (choosing a play, film or TV series that has an overt politically or social message is perhaps a good idea). The producers may also be allotted some given circumstances, and an attitude (again, giving the producers a socio-political identity may help).

Take a well-known play, film, TV series (or scene, or chunk of a scene as above) and make a pitch with a view to having it produced. The idea is to tell the story of the play, film, TV series, with precision, clarity, accuracy and economy. Giving a time limit for the pitch will help.

10: Quotation

Purpose

▶ To remind the actors that they are telling a story.

▶ To encourage them to present that story as something that happened in the past, something that will have had particular consequences and something that could have happened differently – in other words, something that was not inevitable.

Description

The actors 'quote' their lines. After each of their speeches they add the phrase: 'Said the [man/woman/soldier/schoolteacher.]' etc. There is again the possibility for the actor to have an attitude to the character and the action taken. This allows for commentary on the character and action by the actor, and by the company as a whole. Brecht incorporated this technique into the performance script for *The Chalk Circle*, where Simon and Grusha refer to each other and to themselves in the third person as 'the soldier' and 'the lady'.

11: Presenting the Events

Purpose

▶ To develop the ability, in both the actor and the ensemble as a whole, to identify and isolate the key events in a story.

Description

This requires the ensemble as a whole to present the story of an entire play. So familiarity with a suitable play is first necessary (again, choosing a play that has a clear socio-political dimension is advisable). The play needs to have three or four acts (or at least to be divided by the ensemble in this way).

Divide the ensemble into groups (i.e. three or four groups), allocating one act per group. Either during the session or as homework, each group goes through their allocated act identifying the key events (pivotal moments or nodal points) upon which the action of the play turns, and without which the story, as it is, could not progress. Each group then rehearses a short (ten minutes) version of their act that presents just those key dramatic moments to the rest of the ensemble – this must be done with clarity, precision, economy and humour.

There are several different ways of presenting the story. One particularly effective method is to get each group to present their act using a different means of communication. For instance, with a three-act play, Act One could be presented using only 'pictures' (this obviously emphasises 'gestus'), Act Two could be presented using only rhythm (tempo as well as rhythm is an important means of communicating story here), Act Three could be presented using only key words/phrases from the text (for Acts Two and Three in this scenario the rest of the ensemble may close their eyes).

Another fun way of presenting each act (particularly in a drama-school setting) is for each group to use as many aspects of their training as possible to communicate the story, only through these pivotal moments (for instance: Meisner technique, clown, contact impro, stage combat, voice exercises, etc.). If a four-act play has been chosen, the fourth act could be presented in this way. Alternatively, key physical actions could be identified and presented either naturalistically or in a heightened/stylised manner (this could utilise other areas of the student's physical training, such as: Michael Chekhov's 'Psychological Gesture', Meyerhold's 'Biomechanics', Laban or Lecoq, etc.).

12: Sports Commentary

Purpose

▸ To 'objectify' the story or action.
▸ To make the story 'strange'.
▸ To develop a sense of fun in the telling of stories.
▸ To clarify the salient points of a story for a listening (rather than viewing) audience.

Description

Two members of the ensemble become radio sports commentators. They sit to one side of the 'stage', preferably behind a desk, maybe with prop microphones. As the actors act the scene, the commentators give a running commentary of what is happening for the radio audience (i.e. the rest of the company). The actors do not stop playing the scene – the commentary carries on over the top of the action. The aim is for the commentators to 'tell/narrate' the story that is being 'shown' to them. They should aim to communicate the story or action with clarity – their commentary should be objective, precise and entertaining. They should have fun. This exercise may be particularly revealing when characters are involved in an argument, political or otherwise, as this can be commented upon as if it were a boxing match. Greek texts are particularly useful here as the *agon*, or 'combat', is built into the structure of the text. Again, Brecht's *Antigone* is a good example where there is more than one *agon* – Kreon/Antigone and Kreon/Hamon.

ARGUMENT AND CLARITY

Identifying the argument in a scene, and presenting it clearly

13: The Chair of Questions

Purpose

▶ To identify the shifts in argument, status,
   dynamic and agenda.

Description

Take a chunk of text (about two pages) from a scene (must be
a two-hander – again preferably with a socio-political
dimension). The space should be clear except for a single chair,
which is placed centre stage. The scene begins. As soon as one
of the characters asks a question, they firmly place the other
character in the chair. The standing character has command of
the whole space and can move through it as they wish. The
seated character must remain seated until they, in turn, have a
question, whereupon they can get up and, firmly, place the
other character in the chair. The roles are thus reversed until
the seated character has a question, and so on. The argument
or dialectic of the scene is revealed and it becomes clear who
has the status, whose agenda is driving the scene. This is also
useful in terms of establishing a basic 'gestus'.

14: Lawyers and Judge

Purpose

▶ To foreground the argument/dialectic of a scene
   – increasing the awareness in both participating
   actors and observing ensemble of the
   importance of argument for Brechtian theatre.

Description

A member of the ensemble is the judge (alternatively, a small group or the ensemble as a whole can act as the jury). The actors present their scene as lawyers to the judge/jury. They can play the text of the scene as it is, or alternatively they can describe the situation and events of the scene (i.e. narrate). The idea is to persuade the judge/jury of the validity of their argument. This exercise helps to present the argument of the scene with a degree of objectivity, thus mitigating against an excess of emotion that may otherwise blur the political argument that is central to the meaning of the play. Another version of this exercise is to have a marriage counsellor or other form of therapist instead of a judge. There is the option of allotting a particular attitude/identity to the judge/jury – as usual, grounded in a particular socio-political context; even a genuine historical setting: e.g. the Nuremberg Trials; the House Un-American Activities Committee; the South African Truth and Reconciliation Commission; a Sharia court, etc.

Though this exercise is a useful way of exploring any scene that involves an argument of some sort, it may be particularly interesting to work on trial scenes – the final scene of *The Caucasian Chalk Circle*, for example.

15: If, But, Yet...

Purpose

▶ To develop the actor's ability to recognise the way in which an argument is constructed by the playwright – to increase an awareness of the rhetorical dimension of a given text.

Description

Go through the scene (or unit) identifying all the 'connectives' that collectively structure the argument of a speech ('if', 'but', 'yet', 'and', 'so', 'therefore', 'then', 'consequently', etc.). When playing the scene, the actors simply emphasise these 'argument' words – even to the extent that they give these words to the audience, thus breaking the fourth wall (this is particularly effective for scenes that contain longer speeches, e.g. the *agon* section of *Antigone* between Antigone and Kreon, or the duologue between Kreon and Hamon).

16: Shifting the Furniture

Purpose

▶ To increase the actor's awareness of the specific points they are making as part of their argument (this is also useful in terms of identifying dramatic tension or conflict, as expressed in Stanislavsky, through the concept of objective and counter-objective).

Description

In the centre of the space, place as many chairs as possible. The two actors then play the scene freely in the space, each actor allocating one wall as their 'home'. The 'game' is that, every time they make a particular point as part of their persuasive argument, they take a chair from the centre of the room and place it against their wall. A similar exercise is to play a game of draughts or chess, making a move on each new point made.

17: Hand Tower

Purpose

▶ To increase awareness of the argument contained in a scene and the imperative to win that argument – this sense of competition is in keeping with Brecht's love of sport. The physical contact that occurs between the two actors in this exercise is an important addition and helps, particularly, in terms of urgency and dynamic.

Description

The two actors play the scene with their hands in physical contact. Each time a new point is made in the argument (or, alternatively, on every line), the point-scorer places their lower hand on top of the pile of hands (this is useful in relation to continuity of action and dynamic as well as argument). The game is particularly effective (and fun) when played at speed.

18: The Baton of Truth

Purpose

▶ To clarify the shifts in power, status or agenda.
▶ To identify the key points and stages of the argument and so clarify the dialectical nature of the dialogue.

Description

Find something that you can use as a baton, ideally a short stick – but anything will do. It is also possible to use an object which features in the play you're studying, or symbolises what it is the characters are discussing or arguing about – if this object is socially, economically or politically charged in some way, so much the better (the microphone in 'Workers' Playtime' – Scene Thirteen of Fear and Misery of the Third Reich – would be a good example as it symbolises, in a way, control and ownership over the means of communication (or propaganda). The actors then play the scene (as usual, it should be a duologue that has a socio-political dimension – what works particularly well is an overt argument, e.g. Kreon/Antigone). Whoever speaks first has the 'baton of truth' in their hand. The baton either changes hands on every speech – that is, each actor takes the baton every time they have a line – or an actor only takes the baton when they are making a particular point in the argument. The more compelling their point, or the more important it is for them to persuade the other character of the validity of their argument, the more determined they are to take the baton. What is established through this game is 1) the points at which the argument shifts, or the power/status changes, and 2) the need to persuade. In other words, the stakes are highlighted – Kreon is arguing for the city, Antigone for the family; her life is at stake. What should be clarified by this exercise are the key stages of the argument, and also how emotion must not get between the audience and the articulation of that argument.

SOCIAL RELATIONSHIPS

Developing an awareness of the socially determined nature of character and character relationships

19: Social Forces

Purpose

▶ To increase the actor's awareness of the social forces that are at work in a scene, where they exert their power on the characters involved, influencing their behaviour, actions and decisions.

Description

The actors involved in the scene, or the ensemble as a whole, identify the 'forces' (specifically the social forces) that influence the way in which the characters in the scene behave (religious beliefs or background, economic means, class or parentage, job or occupation, age, marital status, health, education, etc.). Appropriate objects are then chosen to represent or symbolise each of these social forces (e.g. a wallet for economic status, a briefcase to represent a businessman/father, a wedding ring to indicate marital status, a wine bottle to represent alcohol dependency, etc.). These objects are then placed around the space, perhaps on chairs. It is helpful if objects representing opposing forces are placed diametrically across the space from each other. The actors then play the scene freely in the space, allowing the objects and the social force that they represent to work on them. Whichever force is having the greatest pull on their attention, and consequently their behaviour, from moment to moment should be the object that they are closest to physically – they may even need to be in actual contact with

the object in question, or they may be pulled equally
between two separate/opposing forces. The actors could
also explore these forces in relation to repulsion as well as
attraction – as if they were powerful magnets exerting either
a positive or negative force on the character.

The conflicts, tensions and social context of the scene
becomes apparent. For Mother Courage these forces would
include each of her children, the cook and his inn in Utrecht,
the Catholic army, the Protestant army, her wagon
(economic means), the war (as both economic condition and
the force that takes her children from her), her social
class/upbringing, etc.

20: Verbalising the Forces

Purpose

▶ As above – but this time through the spoken
  word rather than through the physical body.

Description

Rather than having representative physical objects of the
social forces at work on the two characters, the actors now
simply name those forces repeatedly as they play the scene.
So, to illustrate, if this is the dialogue as written:

TOM: Hello, fancy seeing you here.

CLAIRE: Oh my God, Tom, when did you get back?

TOM: Couple of days ago. Can I get you a drink?

CLAIRE: Well, I can only stay a few minutes, but…

TOM: Great… what would you like?

CLAIRE: Umm… Oh God…

It could now sound something like this (forces that the
actors perceive to be working on their character and which
are being spoken out loud are in *italics*):

TOM: *Lust, lust, lust, lust, etc.* Hello, fancy seeing you here. *Class, class, class, class, schooling, schooling, schooling, lust, lust, etc.*

CLAIRE: *Appearance, appearance, appearance, etc.* Oh my God... *Husband, husband, husband, etc.* Tom, when did you get back?

TOM: *Sex, sex, sex, etc.* Couple of days ago. *Sex, sex, sex.* Can I get you a drink? *Money, money, money, sex, sex, money, money, etc.*

CLAIRE: Well, I can only stay a few minutes, but... *Career, career, career, career, husband, husband, sex, sex, sex, etc.*

TOM: *Class, class, class, family background, family background, sex, sex, sex, etc.* Great... what would you like? *Money, money, money, sex, sex, money, sex, class, etc.*

CLAIRE: *Catholicism, Catholicism, Catholicism, Mother, Mother, sex, sex, sex.* Umm... *Husband, husband, husband, Catholicism, Catholicism, sex, sex, sex, husband, Catholicism, Mother, sex, etc.* Oh God...

The second encounter between Simon and Grusha in the opening scene of *The Caucasian Chalk Circle* is a particularly clear example of a high-stakes situation where two characters are obliged to negotiate their way through a marriage proposal while being affected by a variety of external and internal forces – the coming soldiers (war/danger/fear), the Adjutant and the horses, the third courtyard (social hierarchy/rank), Simon's ten-piasters-a-month wage (economic status), his mother's cross, Grusha's brother (family status), time (urgency), Grusha's right shoulder (health), etc.

The exercise works best if done at speed, without too much intellectualising or deliberation but using knowledge of the play, character and previous identification of social forces to

work spontaneously and instinctively through the actor.
Again, the Brechtian emphasis on fun is essential.

21: Anthropology

Purpose

▶ To increase awareness of the socially
determined nature of character and behaviour –
aiming for a 'scientific objectivity' in the
understanding of character relationships.

Description

Two actors play the scene. Two observing members of the
ensemble are 'anthropologists'. The 'audience' imagines
that the scene being observed is a film, made by
Anthropologist 1, which he or she is showing to
Anthropologist 2. Anthropologist 1 can 'freeze-frame' the
scene at any point in order to explain the behaviour or
actions of the characters involved to his/her colleague.
Anthropologist 2 can ask questions in order to clarify the
socially determined nature of the behaviour/actions on
display. For example:

'Where was [name or title/occupation of character, e.g. 'the
Soldier'] educated?'

Or: 'What is the religious background of the Mother?'

Or: 'How much money does the Schoolteacher have?'

Or: 'How often has Tom had sex at this point?', etc.

Go through the whole scene or a few units of that scene in
order to establish the socialised nature of character, action,
behaviour, choices, status, and so on.

An alternative scenario is to make the two observers
Sherlock Holmes and Dr Watson, for example. After freeze-
framing the scene, Holmes, in pursuit of an 'objective truth'

through observation, comments on each socially specific piece of behaviour/action in the following way:

'Did you notice, Watson, the way in which [observation of behaviour/action], well, that is because [socially determined reason for behaviour/action]'. Watson, like Anthropologist 2, can ask for clarification in order to enhance precision.

22: Just Remind Me

Purpose

▶ As above, but with an increased focus on the particular moment/line – and especially with a view to reminding the actors playing the scene that the nature of their relationship is determined by the social/political/cultural/ historical context of the world that the characters inhabit.

Description

From the ensemble, two 'observers' watch each of the two actors play the scene (one observer per actor). At any point during the scene (particularly at socially/politically charged moments/lines), either observer can stop the scene and ask the actor they have been observing a socially specific question (it is important to use the character's title/ occupation where possible). The question should begin with: 'Just remind me…' For example:

'Just remind me, which newspaper does the Politician read?'

Or: 'Just remind me, at what age did the Road Cleaner leave school?'

Or: 'Just remind me, what political party does the Policeman vote for?', etc.

After the actor has answered the scene continues, unless the observer has further questions in order to clarify matters.

Scene Four of *Galileo* provides a good example of a situation where characters of different rank and social background are brought together with a central point of focus, Galileo's new telescope. These include Galileo's housekeeper Mrs Sarti, her son Andrea, the Grand Duke of Tuscany, Cosimo de Medici, a theologian, Galileo, and Federzoni (a lens-grinder). If working on this scene, observers from the company could stop the action with:

'Just remind me... is the theologian actively involved in looking after the poor?'

Or: 'Just remind me... how much money does Mrs Sarti owe the milkman?'

Or: 'Just remind me... what kind of rent can Federzoni afford with his earnings as a lens-grinder?'

Or: 'Just remind me... how many private buildings do the Medici own?'

Or: 'Just remind me... at what age does a boy of Andrea's class finish school in seventeenth-century Florence?'

Or: 'Just remind me... how much money does Galileo spend on books and how much does he owe other people?'

23: A Hat Full of Archetypes

Purpose

▸ To increase awareness of the socially determined nature of all people.

▸ To increase awareness of how character and behaviour is the result of cultural, historical, social and political contexts.

▸ To show that the individual person is determined by their position in time and place and, unavoidably, sees the world through the prism of their particular place in history.

Description

Compile a list of 'types' relating to occupation or other socially determined identity. These types are written on individual cards which are then placed, face down, in a pile, or, alternatively, on pieces of paper which are then put in a hat. Each member of the ensemble selects a card and then watches a scene (again, a duologue is best – and again preferably a duologue with a socio-political dimension). The workshop leader can 'freeze' the scene at any point – selecting moments of particular socio-political interest. The ensemble has been watching the scene progress from the particular perspective of the social type written on their card – adopting a specific attitude to the action/characters that they are observing.

Examples of types could be: a Liberal mother from Oxford; an Asian bus driver from Bradford; a young man from Surrey training to be an officer at Sandhurst; a Polish immigrant builder living in South East London; a Catholic priest aged eighty from Belfast; a feminist academic from Cardiff working at UCL; an eighteen-year-old boxer from Manchester, etc.

The workshop leader then calls upon one of the observers to comment on the characters/relationships/actions/choices, etc., that they have just witnessed. It is helpful if they begin their commentary with: 'I was shocked/amazed/appalled/ surprised/unsettled (or equivalent) by the way that [give details of characters' behaviour and actions]'. It is, in particular, a question of how characters have behaved, how they have acted, how they have responded to events, that is important in relation to the Brechtian prioritising of the how/why things happen the way they do – as opposed to the 'what happens next' of dramatic rather than epic or dialectic theatre.

GESTUS

Conveying meaning through the stage picture

24: Changing the Gaze

Purpose

▶ To highlight the way in which a simple change to
a particular aspect of the 'gestus' changes the
nature of the socially determined relationship
and, in turn, changes the way in which the
audience receives/understands the story and
what that story means.

Description

Play the unit, group of units, or whole scene through several
times. First: character A is *always* looking at character B,
while character B is *never* looking at character A. Then
reverse this. Then try the scene with both characters always
looking at each other. Then with neither character looking at
the other. Then go back to the first exercise (character A
always looking at B, while B is *never* looking at A), only this
time an 'observer' calls 'Change!' at various moments during
the scene (perhaps the politically or socially charged
moments). On 'Change!' the characters/actors swap (i.e. A is
now *never* looking at B, while B is *always* looking at A).

The ensemble can explore other permutations in relation to
the gaze. This exercise is very interesting in relation to
power, status, class, and the socially determined nature of
the relationship and circumstances of the scene – in other
words, the scene's 'gestus'. Scene Three of *Fear and Misery
of the Third Reich*, 'The Chalk Cross', can be explored

productively in this way, dependent as it is upon the status/rank/gender of the characters in it, particularly in relation to the SA Man.

25: Sculpture

Purpose

▶ To increase awareness of the need for physical precision in the formation of stage pictures through the position and shape of the actor's body, and through the physical relationship between actors in the space. In other words: to highlight the importance of the 'gestus' in the communication of the meaning, specifically social meaning, which is intrinsic to the dramaturgical structure and socio-political content of the play/scene.

Description

The two actors play the units, group of units, or whole scene. An 'observer' shouts, 'Freeze!' Two or more 'sculptors' then 'sculpt' the two actors – moving them in relation to each other and to the space, as well as simply changing their physical shape. Other members of the ensemble may call out instructions in order to further define the gestic stage picture, aiming for precision, clarity and simplicity in the physical story of the scene/relationship. The actors then continue the scene, starting where they left off, from the new physical shape and spatial dynamic. This starting and stopping may be repeated as the scene progresses. As usual, it is helpful if the observer who stops the scene does so at politically or socially charged moments. This exercise may be particularly useful when exploring scenes where the characters involved represent very different physical types, for instance, Scene Six of *Galileo*, where a group of monks and scholars of different shapes, sizes and ages await Clavius's verdict on Galileo's telescope and its implications in relation to the Ptolemaic model of the cosmos.

26: Linking the Pictures

Purpose

▶ To increase awareness of the importance of communicating key dramatic moments within the story through the stage picture (paying particular attention to the nodal points or pivotal moments), and to develop the ability to identity these moments.

▶ To highlight the socially conditioned nature of the relationship between the characters in terms of the scene's 'gestus'.

Description

The two actors first go through the unit, group of units, or whole scene identifying moments within the dramatic action where the socio-political significance of each of those moments, and the socially conditioned nature of the relationship between the two characters, may be illuminated through the precise shaping of the stage picture. When these moments (a maximum of five is probably a good idea) have been identified, the two actors work on the specifics of a stage picture which will communicate that particular moment of action most effectively. Moments of exchange, particularly economic transactions, are especially effective – the moment when Olga gives Andrey the 'little key' to the cupboard in Act Three of Chekhov's *Three Sisters* is a good example, or when the Old Peasant finally gives Grusha the milk for baby Michael in *The Caucasian Chalk Circle*.

Again it may help if 'observers' aid them in the precise details of the physical picture, either through suggestion or through physically 'sculpting', as in the previous exercise. Once the ensemble is satisfied that these key stage pictures clearly articulate with precision, economy and simplicity the socio-political meaning of that particular moment in relation to the dramaturgy of the scene/play as a whole, then the actors run the unit/sequence of units/scene ensuring that they include, at the appropriate moment and as precisely as possible, each of the physical pictures. The resulting performance should convey the socio-political meaning of the scene, at least in part, through these physical pictures – through the comportment of the characters/actors and the way in which they relate to each other and to the space within the historically specific social context that is intrinsic to the world of the play.

27: Is That How...?

Purpose

▶ To challenge any unexamined assumptions or clichéd representation of behaviour by the actor.

Description

Again, 'observers' watch the behaviour of the two actors who play the scene (with one observer allocated to each actor). Either observer can stop the scene at any point and ask the actor a question that always begins: 'Is that how...?' It should always refer to a particular action and to the character's social identity. So, for instance:

'Is that how a policeman whose pension is being threatened and is facing possible redundancy because of government cuts to the police budget shakes hands with the visiting Conservative Home Secretary?'

Or: 'Is that how the mother of a soldier killed in Iraq receives a compensation cheque for £600 from a military official following a long court proceeding?'

Or: 'Is that how a young civilian man from the Syrian town of Homs sits on a chair (with Emily Maitlis on one side and a female academic on the other) in the *Newsnight* TV studio, while making a plea to the British people for military aid?'

The actor must then adapt his or her behaviour, particularly in relation to their physical life, in order to clarify the 'gestus' at this point in the action. Exchanges or transactions of some kind, particularly those involving money, are especially powerful – the importance of economic context to the functioning of human relationships is central to Brechtian theory. (Brecht used a version of this exercise while working on *Mother Courage*: 'This is how a woman stands who is pretending not to recognise the body of her son so that she can maintain her business.')

28: Silent Movie

Purpose

▶ To highlight the importance of communicating the story of the play through the stage picture.

▶ To emphasise the need for economy, precision, simplicity and clarity.

Description

The ensemble goes through the scene and identifies the key events. They then decide upon titles for these events emphasising their socio-political significance. In *Mother Courage*, written titles detailing the main action of the scene that was about to be shown were displayed for the audience to read – e.g. 'Mother Courage at the peak of her business career' (John Willett's translation). These titles are written down on pieces of card or paper large enough to be seen by the whole ensemble when held up. One 'narrator' takes responsibility for these cards. Two 'silent movie stars' are chosen from the ensemble. The narrator, silent movie stars

and the two actors then show the rest of the ensemble the
scene in the following way: the narrator holds up the first
card that gives the title of the first event; the actors begin to
act the scene; and, next to them, the silent movie stars form
the appropriate physical pictures that demonstrate the action
as it unfolds. It is important that they don't feel the need to
demonstrate too many pictures, just the important ones that
tell the story, and it is essential that they do this, as usual, with
clarity, precision, simplicity and economy. When a new event
begins, the narrator holds up the relevant card. In addition to
'gestus', the Brechtian formal use of montage is introduced.

29: A Series of Meetings

Purpose

▶ To highlight the fact that people behave
  differently depending on who they are with.
▶ To demonstrate that their behaviour and their
  relationships are sociallly/politically/
  economically/culturally determined.
▶ Furthermore, that this behaviour can be
  expressed physically through the character's
  'comportment', and that the resulting picture is
  gestic in nature.

Description

This exercise is designed to be used when a group is
working together on a whole play. Each actor can have a go
at the exercise in order to explore all the relationships that
their character has in the play – focusing on each relationship
in terms of its 'gestus'. Using either scenes from the play or
improvised situations, the actor explores their character's
behaviour or attitude (which may be contradictory, in that
they behave differently in different circumstances and with
different people) in relation to each of the other characters.
Improvised scenarios should aim to create situations that

have a particular social, economic, political or cultural dimension. For instance, we could see the same man (for example, a lower-middle-class Catholic, thirty-five years old, struggling financially, from Hull) with, alternately: his wife, his fifteen-year-old son, his seven-year-old daughter, his bank manager, his boss, his best friend in the pub, his mistress, his priest, the new recruit at work who makes the tea, his father, the visiting Conservative candidate who went to Eton, etc.

In *The Good Person of Szechwan*, Brecht created Shui Ta, the alter ego of his female protagonist Shen Teh. In doing so, he followed to its logical conclusion the idea that a person's comportment changes dependent upon who they are talking to, and the nature of that particular relationship in socio-economic terms.

The aim of the exercise is to find the 'gestus' particular to that relationship – the differences in the actor's comportment, gesture, gaze, walk, etc., could be exaggerated in order to explore those differences fully. Again, it may help if an 'observer' or the viewing ensemble as a whole offer suggestions or physically sculpt the actor in order to increase clarity/precision. When the company is happy that the most expressive gestic picture has been created, someone could take a picture on their phone to show the actor. Taking photographs of the gestic pictures created in all of the exercises in this section is a good idea and something Brecht did himself for inclusion in his Model Books.

ALIENATION

Seeing the familiar in new ways

30: Say That Again!

Purpose

▶ To ensure that both actors and the rest of the ensemble *really hear* key lines and words in the text. In particular that they hear the socially or politically charged utterances of the characters in relation to the socio-political context of the scene or play. This should result in familiar phrases or expressions being heard in a new way and, as a result, being made strange.

Description

The two actors play the scene. Every time either actor hears a phrase that is socially or politically loaded – that in some way may reveal the socio-economic class of the speaker and the socially determined assumptions that they hold – then they ask the other actor to: 'Say that again.' The actor must then repeat the phrase. If the receiving actor is still 'shocked' by the phrase, then they can repeat the request. This continues until both actors and audience have *really heard* the socially/politically significant phrase.

An example might be: a chauffeur is driving a rich businessman to a conference, and during the conversation the businessman may mention that the evening meal, which they are to be provided with, cost £4,000.

CHAUFFEUR: Say that again.

BUSINESSMAN: The meal cost £4,000.

CHAUFFEUR: Say that again!

BUSINESSMAN: It cost £4,000.

The whole scene is played highlighting these socially/ politically charged moments in this way, thus making them strange. Moments in a play which feature money are especially revealing, exposing as they do the economic forces at play in the particular character relationship under scrutiny. There are numerous examples from Brecht: the haggling over the value of a scrawny capon in Scene Two of *Mother Courage* – a value which rises when the General and Eilif demand meat – is particularly memorable and a good example of market forces in action at the domestic level. (I'm also reminded of all the talk of money that is at the heart of Chekhov's *The Cherry Orchard*, and which is linked directly to attitudes that are inextricably associated with social class.)

31: Tag Acting

Purpose

▶ To draw attention to behaviour that is, at least to some degree, socially determined. For instance: behaviour that is specifically linked to gender, race/ethnicity, class or socio-economic background.

Description

In addition to the two actors who are in the scene, a further two actors are allocated as their 'tag-team partners'. The scene begins and each partner observes their actor. Whenever they wish, they can 'tag' their actor and take over from them in the scene from that point in the action. From attentive observation of their actor, they aim to replicate their behaviour, physicality, voice, idiosyncrasies, mannerisms, etc., as accurately as possible. It is particularly revealing if the partner belongs to a different/contrasting social group from the actor that they observe, for example, a woman observes a man or vice versa.

After the original actor has spent some time observing their own behaviour reflected in the performance of their partner, they in turn can tag them and re-enter the scene, this time attempting to replicate what they have observed. They are now playing a version of themselves – their habitual behaviour has been made strange to both them and to the observing ensemble as a whole. This tagging, involving both pairs, continues through the scene – consequently there is the possibility of four different pairings.

This exercise would, perhaps, be particularly useful for an actress playing Shen Teh in *The Good Person of Szechwan*, if her tag partner was male. Also for an actor playing Mr Puntila in *Mr Puntila and his Man Matti*, in order to explore the two contrasting comportments, one for the 'cold sober' and one for the 'friendly drunk' side of his character. This game could also be played with larger scenes, possibly even involving the whole company, e.g. seven original actors and seven tag partners.

32: Challenge the Audience

Purpose

▶ To draw the attention of the audience (in this case, the rest of the ensemble) to the significant phrases in the scene, in relation to political and socio-economic context and the social status of the speaker.

Description

The actors go through the unit/scene and identify the socially/politically charged phrases that their characters utter. They then play the scene. Each time they come to one of these phrases, they address it directly to the audience. Alternatively, they could turn to the audience and look at them for a beat following their delivery of the phrase, before returning their attention to the onstage action.

This breaks the fourth wall and also implicates the audience in the action of the play, endowing them with an identity as a political/social entity, particular to the historical context of the moment – they are, in other words, challenged to adopt an attitude to the onstage world and the choices made by the characters in that world. The actors here are effectively commenting on the behaviour of the characters that they are playing. There is also the opportunity in this exercise to give the observing ensemble a 'collective' (possibly historically based) identity. A group of monks/cardinals, for instance, watching Galileo demonstrate the effectiveness of his new telescope, while explaining the potential implications.

33: Alter Egos

Purpose

▶ To highlight the socially determined nature of both the characters in the scene and the relationship between those characters. (Often degrees of hypocrisy are exposed.)

Description

This is another version of the 'Quotation' exercise (see Exercise 10, above), but using four people rather than two. Each of the two actors is allocated an 'alter ego' (i.e. another member of the ensemble). As the actors play the scene, the two alter egos follow them round the space commenting on what they do and say directly to the audience. For example:

ACTOR 1: What do you mean, you can't come to Paris for the weekend?

ALTER EGO OF ACTOR 1: Said the stockbroker with a four-bedroom flat in Chelsea.

ACTOR 2: I'd love to, I really would... but...

ALTER EGO OF ACTOR 2: Said the unemployed actor who lives in a bedsit in Crouch End.

Or:

ACTOR 1: Would you like to stay the night?

ALTER EGO OF ACTOR 1: Said the millionaire octogenarian, while sipping his/her glass of Dom Pérignon.

ACTOR 2: Well... I'm not sure... it is rather late...

ALTER EGO OF ACTOR 2: Said the unemployed actor, while checking her/his bus timetable.

The scene is played in this way to the end. Again, the audience is made to look at the scene afresh through being made aware of the social context that determines the nature of the relationship.

34: Stand-up Commentary

Purpose

▶ To explore Brecht's conviction that the most effective way to comment upon social inequality and human contradiction is through humour. This kind of commentary is intended to act in a parallel way to the Brechtian device of stopping the dramatic action in order for the actors to sing a song that comments on that action.

Description

A panel of 'politically engaged comedians' (representing views across the political spectrum) stand in a line watching the two actors play the scene, while the rest of the ensemble watch both the actors and the comedians. The

comedians act as a kind of chorus who comment on the
action directly to and for the benefit of the audience – a bit
like Statler and Waldorf, the two old men sat in balcony seats
in *The Muppets*.

Whenever they wish, a comedian may 'buzz', thus freezing
the scene. They then proceed to give a short comic routine
that in some way comments on what has just been observed
– commenting on characters, action, situation, text, etc., in
relation to political, social or economic ideas (often
demonstrating a particularly biased viewpoint/attitude). As
soon as they finish their routine/commentary and step back in
line, the action continues. Another member of the ensemble
could keep score or award points for each interjection.

MOMENTS OF DECISION

Showing how things could be different

35: Not That, But This

Purpose

▶ To alert the actors and the observing ensemble to the possibility, implicit in every choice that a character makes, that an alternative choice could have been made. The events that are dramatised in the play, including the choices/decisions made by individual characters, are *not* inevitable – the things that happened in the past need *not*, necessarily, have happened. This in turn leads to the Brechtian/Marxist assertion that the world need not be the way it is – that change is possible, and that change in the real world can be effected through art. A particularly clear demonstration of this 'moment of choice' is the dramatically extended end to Scene One, 'The Noble Child', in *The Caucasian Chalk Circle*, where Grusha has to decide whether or not to take baby Michael with her to the mountains. Another powerful example that springs to mind is the moment of choice at the end of Arthur Miller's *The Crucible*, when Proctor has to decide whether or not to sign his name to the 'confession', which he has been coerced into making. The play itself is, of course, a striking instance of the use of an historical

event as parable/analogue, in order to
comment upon a current political situation. In
Mother Courage, Brecht uses the Thirty Years
War to similar effect, while in *The Resistible
Rise of Arturo Ui* he constructs a fictional world,
based on 1930s gangland Chicago, to satirise
the rise of Hitler in Nazi Germany.

Description

During the playing of the scene, each actor comments on the
choices their character makes at each moment of decision,
whether explicit or implied. They do this using the social
identity of the character and phrasing the decision using the
past tense. So for example [commentary in *italics*]:

LORD SMITH: Come here and kiss me.

MARIA: *The Eastern European servant girl did **not** walk out
of the room (slap LORD SMITH/scream for help/laugh in
his face, etc.) **but** instead walked over to him and,
reluctantly, kissed him as asked:* Yes, sir.

This type of commentary, using what Brecht referred to as
the 'not… but', is employed every time the actor perceives
that the character they are playing is faced with a choice –
particularly if the social/political implications of that choice
are central to the themes of the play. In *Galileo*, when
Cardinal Bellarmin confronts Galileo with: 'You come along
and accuse this Higher Being [i.e. God] of not being quite
clear how the stars move, whereas you yourself are. Is that
sensible?' Galileo does **not** answer: 'Yes, it is sensible; I have
seen the movement of the stars with my own eyes through
my telescope.' **But** instead replies: 'I am a faithful son of the
church…' (John Willett's translation).

36: Interrogation

Purpose

▶ To highlight the socio-economic reasons that lie behind the choices a character makes.

Description

An 'interrogator' (or a panel of interrogators) are elected from the ensemble. As the actors play the scene, the interrogator stops the action when he/she perceives a choice to have been made by either of the characters and asks them why they made that choice rather than an alternative or opposite choice. As usual, the interrogator must phrase the question using the social identity of the character and referring to the action in the past tense. The actor responds giving reasons that relate to the social/political/economic/ historical context in which the character lives. For example:

INTERROGATOR: Why did the soldier choose to rape the girl?

SOLDIER: Because he had become brutalised by the foreign war and had come to see the ethnic group that the girl came from as not really human – particularly since the previous day, when the girl's brother was part of an insurgent group that had shot at his battalion, fatally wounding his best friend.

This interrogation continues through the scene, questions being levelled at each character at every moment perceived by the interrogator/s to represent a choice. In the opening scene of Brecht's *Antigone*, Ismene tries to persuade her sister to 'forget the past'. Antigone insists that the reason Ismene can suggest such a thing is because she is younger and has witnessed less horror – 'when we forget the past the past returns' (Judith Malina's translation).

37: Show Me the Alternative

Purpose

▶ To demonstrate the Brechtian emphasis on the possibility of alternative choices – that what happened was not inevitable.

Description

As with the exercise above, the 'interrogator/s' stop the scene when they perceive a choice to have been made by a character. This time, the interrogator simply says: 'Show me what else the social identity [teacher, student, nurse, doctor, mother, brother, etc.] could have done.' The actors then improvise the scene that could have transpired had the character made another – or, most powerfully, the opposite – choice. The interrogator/s decide when to end the improvisation. The actors then return to where they were in the scene and continue until the next moment of choice.

At the end of the exercise, it is useful if the ensemble discuss the ultimate consequences of the various choices made by the characters. This fosters in the ensemble an awareness of the Brechtian contention that the unfolding of history in a particular way was not/is not inevitable – that social and political change is possible. A similar device is used by Brecht in *The Caucasian Chalk Circle* when The Singer tells us what Grusha and Simon 'thought but did not say' at the end of the first half of the play just before Azdak's entrance (Eric Bentley's translation).

38: What Would You Do?

Purpose

▶ To highlight the possibility of alternative choices.

▶ To mitigate against a sense of inevitability in relation to the unfolding action of the play. Here the focus is on attitudes held by the individual

members of the ensemble – the idea is to foster
a developed political and social consciousness in
the ensemble as a collective.

Description

The two actors playing the scene first go through the text
and identify the moments where they perceive a choice to
have been made by their character. They then play the
scene, stopping at the moment of choice, turning to the
audience and asking them directly: 'What would you have
done?' (Once again it is important to use the past tense.)
This is reminiscent of the despairing cry of the tragic hero in
ancient Greek drama: *'Oi moi, ti drasso'* – 'Alas, what must I
do?' – almost certainly directed out to the audience (itself a
political entity).

The discussion that follows should expose prejudices,
assumptions and attitudes in the ensemble, which are socially
determined. The workshop leader can guide the debate in
such a way that the socially determined nature of
relationships and the behaviour of individuals within a
specific historical and cultural context is emphasised.

Alternatively, rather than saying: 'What would you have
done?', the exercise can be explored less discursively if the
actor says *'Show me* what you would have done.' Again,
individual ensemble members can demonstrate what they
think they would have done, as themselves, in that situation
(this is, in fact, making use of the Stanislavskian 'magic if'). Or
each ensemble member can have been alloted a particular
socio-political identity beforehand – perhaps by using the
'Hat Full of Archetypes' (see Exercise 23, above). This
exercise would work particularly well with Scene Two of
Fear and Misery of the Third Reich, 'A Case of Betrayal'. Here,
a married couple are listening at their front door as a
neighbour is dragged out of his flat and down the stairs –
they do nothing. The actors playing this short scene turn to

the audience at each key moment and ask them: 'What
would you have done?'

39: Give Me the Reasons

Purpose

▶ To expose as many of the reasons as possible,
within the particular social context of the play,
that collectively contribute to a particular choice
being made by a particular character at a
particular moment in their lives.

Description

This time, the 'interrogator/s' stop the scene at perceived
moments of choice/decision and ask the actor in question:
'Why did [the soldier, scientist, dentist, father, etc.] make
(past tense) that choice?' Alternatively, the question may be
phrased negatively: 'Why *didn't* the [...] make the choice to
[here the interrogator can come up with an alternative
possibility – or, most powerfully, articulate the opposite
choice]?' The actor must then list the reasons that they
believe lie behind the choice (it may be helpful for the
interrogator to steer them towards reasons that relate to
the social/political/economic influences on their lives). If the
interrogator considers the answers given to be insufficient
they can suggest additional causes that may lie behind the
choice. Again, a debate may ensue – though this should be
kept brief. Following the interrogation the scene resumes
from the same point.

CONTRADICTION/COMPLEX SEEING

Showing the contradictions of history, society and the individual

40: Internal Soundtrack

Purpose

▶ To expose the fact that human beings exhibit many characteristics – characteristics that are often antagonistic and lie in opposition to each other, causing internal tensions. Such contradictory tendencies, when isolated and focused upon, can result in diametrically opposed readings of a scene.

Description

Having spent time analysing both the play as a whole and their character in relation to the play, the actors select two pieces of music, which represent opposing characteristics (the evidence for which should be demonstrably present in the text). The choice of music should be personal and evoke in the actor feelings that correspond to the characteristics identified. For instance, the character may be demonstrably 'hot-headed' and prone to violence, while also being capable of acts of great tenderness. The point is that different circumstances – social, economic, political – produce contradictory behaviour in any individual.

The actors then show the scene while simultaneously listening to either piece of music through headphones. They then repeat the exercise playing the other piece of music that they have chosen. There are four possible 'meetings' of music that can take place. Each combination should produce a different scene. What is affected by the musical underscores is the mood/atmosphere, the tempo-rhythm, the emotional life, etc. (these terms are more usually associated with Stanislavsky but, I would argue, equally applicable in a Brechtian context).

41: On the One Hand This, On the Other Hand That

Purpose

▸ To expose the contradictions in operation at a particular moment in the play – highlighting the struggle that a character may be experiencing at that particular moment.

Description

Once again, events that occur during the action which bear the most scrutiny are those that relate to moments of choice. At these moments, the actors should stop the scene and articulate the particular dilemma, highlighting the contradictions involved. They should, as usual, describe their character in the third person with reference to social identity and using the past tense. The same wording should frame the articulation of each perceived contradiction – 'On the one hand... while on the other hand...' For example:

'On the one hand the businessman was at this point a millionaire, while on the other hand he was brought up in the ghetto during the Second World War.'

Or: 'On the one hand the serial killer enjoyed torturing his victims, while on the other hand he was kind towards his pets.'

Or: 'On the one hand the gangster was honest, loyal and just towards his family and friends, while on the other hand he robbed banks and shot at the police without the slightest sense of guilt.'

Or: 'On the one hand Mother Courage wants to protect her children from the dangers of war, on the other hand she follows the army into battle in order to make a living from the war.'

Following this explanation, the scene continues from the same point until another moment of choice, where contradictory forces are at work, is identified. The use of 'interrogators' may help to clarify the contradictory nature of the world of the play, and of the human characters within the particular set of social conditions that make up that world. Actors and the observing ensemble develop a way of 'seeing' character, relationship, action and choice that is increasingly 'complex'. That is to say, there is a growing sensitivity to the contradictions and contingencies that are present in any event when observed closely in relation to the social/economic/political/historical/cultural context in which it takes place.

42: I Think This, Whereas I Do That

Purpose 42.1

▶ To explore the potential contradiction between what a character may *think/feel/believe* on the one hand and what they *do* on the other.

Purpose 42.2

▶ To explore the separation of actor from character – looking to highlight the actor's attitude to the behaviour/choices of the character that they are playing.

Description 42.1

The actors should identify the moments of choice/decision/ tension/struggle/contradiction for their character. They play the scene, stopping at these key moments and voicing the contradiction, this time in the following way: 'The thief/

magistrate/priest/daughter at this point *felt/thought/ believed* [give a short precise description] whereas what they *did* was…' The actors then show what it was that the characters did. (Galileo's actions, particularly his public actions, are often at odds with his beliefs in *Galileo*.)

Description 42.2

In the second stage of the exercise, the actors describe at each juncture what it is, in the present tense and from their contemporary perspective, that they, the actor, *feel/think /believe* about what the character *did* (in the past tense) – which they then go on to show/dramatise. In this way, the actor comments on (judges, even) the behaviour/action/ decision of the character they are playing from their own perspective, which is, of course, just as historically/culturally/ socially determined as that of the character.

43: Contradictory Epithets

Purpose

▶ To highlight the contradictory nature of human beings: where Stanislavsky (following Aristotle) emphasised coherent and logical consistency of character – in terms of psychology, behaviour and action – Brecht emphasised the inherent contradictions in both the human being and the world at large.

Description

This exercise requires a good knowledge of the play as a whole and the relationship of each character to the dramaturgical structure of the play, as well as their social identity within the historicised context of that particular world. Having analysed their character within the context of the play as a whole, the actors decide upon three titles or epithets that represent contrasting aspects of their character – it is essential that these titles are derived directly from the text. The titles should refer to contrasting types of behaviour demonstrated at different points in the play. These behaviours may well appear to be inconsistent because the character is in relation to different sets of circumstances, and is involved in different socially conditioned relationships at different points in the story. A good example can be found in *The Good Person of Szechwan*, where Yang Sun behaves very differently (to the extent that he seems like two distinct characters) depending on whether he is with Shen Teh or Shui Ta.

Examples of titles are: The Dashing Pilot, The Attentive Lover, The Compulsive Liar, The Faithless Friend, The Angry Tyrant, The Noble Hero, The Rebellious Son, The City's Saviour, The Proud Ruler, The Arrogant Egotist, The Lonely Foreigner (the first four could refer to Yang Sun, the last seven could describe Oedipus). Select three such contrasting titles for each character. The actors begin the scene focusing their performance on one title only.

At any point in the action, an 'observer' shouts: 'Change!' The actors then continue the scene from that point but switch to another of the three characteristics that they have previously identified. As the scene progresses in this way, the observer can call for one or other of the characters to change, rather than both. In this way, there is the possibility of nine different pairings – and each time the scene should be different (there is also the possibility of dictating the style of performance, e.g. naturalistic, melodramatic, silent movie, film noir, romantic comedy, etc.).

44: Jekyll and Hyde

Purpose

▸ To highlight the contradictions inherent in any
  human being. Here the emphasis is on a more
  pronounced duality or polarisation of
  characteristics – 'good' and 'evil'.

▸ To explore the moral dimension of the scene –
  emphasising the socio-politial forces and
  situations at work on a character.

▸ To demonstrate how 'character' is not fixed but
  dependent upon situation/circumstances and the
  power of external forces.

Description

This exercise again requires a good knowledge of the
play/character that is being worked on. As in the previous
exercise, the actors go through the text identifying key
characteristics/behaviours/attitudes that their character
displays (they must take these characteristics directly from
the text). This time, those characteristics/behaviours/
attitudes should be divided into 'good/virtues' on the one
hand, and 'bad/vices' on the other. The character is now
understood as 'contradictory/dualistic' – a Jekyll and Hyde
figure (the Shen Teh/Shui Ta, and the sober/drunk Puntila are
the obvious models from Brecht).

The actors then play the scene as either 'Jekyll' or 'Hyde'. An
'observer' (or two observers, one attached to each
character) calls out 'Change!' at intervals – the actors then
switch to the opposite set of characteristics/behaviours/
attitudes. As usual, it helps if the observers choose moments
that are politically/socially charged. There are four possible
character meetings, all of which should produce a different
scene – and perhaps help to show the familiar in a new,
estranged, way.

45: Body Versus Voice

Purpose

▶ To demonstrate the notion of contradiction through the expressive tools of body and voice.

▶ To look at the possibility of communicating the contradictory nature of the individual through the power of a single expressive moment.

▶ Also to have fun!

Description

The actors explore, playfully, ways of creating character though oppositions between voice and body. Some examples: A fast, physical tempo-rhythm coupled with a slow, measured vocal delivery, and vice versa; a heavy, earthy, 'masculine' physicality coupled with a high, airy 'feminine' voice, and vice versa; a confident, laid-back, relaxed physicality, coupled with a tense, held, nervous vocal quality, and vice versa. Experimenting with accents can also be revealing here – particularly in relation to perceptions/assumptions of class in connection with provenance. A secondary purpose here is to develop a playful, humorous way of working and to wind down the session before going into the 'round-up' exercises, following.

COMPANY ROUND-UP/APPROACHING THE PLAY

Seeing character as part of a specific set of circumstances, where relationships and behaviour are governed by cultural forces particular to the historical moment

46: Speed-dating

Purpose

▶ To help a cast, working on a particular play, to understand at a deeper level the socially determined nature of the relationships between characters in that play. This is particularly useful where relationships in the play are significant but where the characters in question do not have a great deal of dialogue together (once more, in addition to Brecht's own plays, there are many useful examples from Chekhov and Shakespeare).

Description 46.1

The space is set up as if for a speed-dating event (chairs in pairs facing each other with some distance between each pair). Every character takes a chair. The workshop leader blows a whistle, rings a bell, or shouts: 'Go' – each pair of characters quiz each other to see how socially compatible they are.

The questions they ask each other should relate specifically to the cultural/political/social/economic forces that define character. So, for example: Where do you go to school? What paper do you read? How much money do you earn? What car do you drive? Are you religious? What party do you vote for? Where do you live – in a mansion, house, flat, bedsit?, etc.

After precisely one minute the workshop leader blows the whistle and everyone changes partners. This continues – each conversation lasting one minute – until all characters in the play have met each other. This should be followed by a company discussion where any insights, relating specifically to the socially determined nature of these relationships, are examined collectively by the ensemble. In a drama-school setting, where it is often the case that roles are divided between actors, it can be very informative (and sometimes very funny) to see what happens when two actors playing the same character meet each other! Would Mother Courage like herself if she met herself face to face? Also, such a meeting can point to interesting contradictions if the two actors have a different take on the character in question.

Description 46.2

The same, only this time the workshop leader introduces topics of conversation that the dating couples have to discuss, for example, politics, religion, education, sex, money, class, etc.

47: Focus Group

Purpose

▶ To help clarify the socially determined attitudes held by the different characters in a play to the events that occur in that play.

Description

Either one of the actors or the workshop leader directs a forum (a community hall may be a useful setting to imagine), asking key questions that relate directly to the events of the play. The characters are encouraged to discuss the events from their own particular, socially conditioned, perspective.

The aim is to increase awareness within the ensemble of the social differences, tensions, contradictions and potential conflicts that are inherent in the social nexus of this particular world.

A further exercise (and one that is Brechtian in that it relates/contrasts the world of the play, which exists in the past, to the contemporary world of the actors) is to get the actors, *as themselves*, to comment on the events of the play from their own historicised and socially determined perspective.

Finally, once again in character, each individual could be asked to comment on some contemporary event (the London Riots, for example, or the cuts, or the War on Terror, or *The X-Factor*, or phone hacking, or the 2012 Olympics, or gay marriage), thus bringing the ensemble's attention to their own society and political situation.

48: Contemporary Images

Purpose

▶ A quick-fire game that involves the whole ensemble physically and attempts to incorporate simply, economically and as precisely as possible the ideas relating to epic theatre as explored through the exercises outlined above.

Description

The workshop leader has previously come up with a number of current events of social/political/economic/historical/cultural significance. In addition to this, they have conceived of a number of groups, defined by their social identity. Both events and social groups could be written on cards, which are then placed face down in two separate piles. The workshop leader selects a card from each pile and reads out the event and the social group. The ensemble then has to create a tableau, as quickly as possible, that shows the attitude or 'gestus' of this particular socially defined group in relation to the contemporary event named. So, for example:

The Metropolitan Police demonstrate their attitude to the phone-hacking scandal.

Or: Members of UKIP demonstrate their attitude to the potential collapse of the Eurozone.

Or: A group of A-level students demonstrate their attitude to the rise of university fees to £9,000 per year.

The point is to create, collectively, stage pictures that express with accuracy, economy, simplicity, clarity and precision a particular socially determined attitude or 'gestus' that communicates to an imagined audience a particular idea or story.

49: Tribes

Purpose

▶ To draw attention to the social/cultural groupings that underpin, and to a greater or lesser extent define, the relationships between individuals in this particular ensemble.

Description 49.1

The workshop leader asks the group to walk freely around the space. After a few moments, they call out a category relating to a particular, socially determined identity, e.g. gender, race, class, religion, sexual orientation, age group, musical taste, wealth, schooling, etc. Everybody has to then get into groups based on that category – these groups may be obvious (i.e. male and female) or require some discussion (if the category is religion then groups may, for instance, include Catholics, Muslims, Hindus, Atheists, Agnostics, etc., or simply believers and non-believers).

It is important that discussion should be kept to a minimum
and should be conducted swiftly and with a sense of fun/play.
Alternatively, oppositional pairings could be called out by the
workshop leader and the ensemble should instantly divide
themselves into two groups accordingly, e.g. state school or
private school; middle class or working class; employed or
unemployed; born here or born abroad; member of a politial
party or not; in credit or overdrawn; over thirty or under
thirty, etc. These social groupings can be sensitive, so the
ensemble should be well established before trying this
exercise.

Description 49.2

The same, only this time as the characters they are playing, if
the company is rehearsing a play.

50: Top to Bottom

Purpose

▶ This is a status game designed to identify the
  various hierarchies or 'pecking orders' at work
  within a particular social group. It is an exercise
  that is designed to explore the complex social
  relationships that exist in a play – again it could be
  played with the actors as themselves, though this
  would require a great deal of trust and sensitivity.

Description

The actors walk around the room in character. After a few
moments, the workshop leader calls out a particular
category beginning their sentence with 'The most...' So, for
instance: 'The most wealthy.' The actors then line
themselves up, right to left, from the most to least wealthy –
this is according to their reading of the play and
understanding of their character's social position in relation
to the other characters.

Other categories might be: most good-looking, clever, intelligent, privileged, loved, hated, educated, right-/left-wing, sexually experienced, dangerous, happy, wealthy, hopeful, bitter, etc. This is particularly fascinating, and can be extremely revealing, when characters disagree over their social ranking in relation to a particular category and in relation to the other characters.

Once more, it is particularly informative if a role is divided between actors. Differences of opinion as to where a character sits within the social hierarchy of the play, relative to other characters, can spark interesting debates and often reveal contradictions that may be demonstably present in the text.

The game could be played once with the actors deciding upon their ranking from the perspective of the character inside the play, then again from the actor's own objective view of their character, from the outside. This is a useful way of the actor formulating an 'attitude' to the character they are playing. Again it is essential that the game is played at speed and with a sense of fun – not too much thinking time!

An alternative version is to play this game while rehearsing a scene – when the workshop leader calls out the category, rather than forming a line, the actors continue playing the scene but adjust their *height* in the room according to status, e.g. the 'most ruthless' character has to make sure that they are the tallest/highest/straightest in the room, while the least ruthless has to be the shortest/lowest/most bent. This could end up with people standing on chairs or tables or lying flat on the floor – once more an instant gestic picture, based on a particular social hierarchy, is created.

A practical, hands-on guide – for actors, directors, teachers and students – to Brecht's theory and practice of theatre.

The Complete Brecht Toolkit examines, one by one, Brecht's many, sometimes contradictory ideas about theatre – and how he put them into practice. Here are explanations of all the famous key terms, such as **Alienation Effect, Epic Theatre** and **Gestus**, as well as the many others which go to make up what we think of as 'Brechtian theatre'.

There follows a section which looks at the practical application of these theories in Acting, Language, Music, Design and Direction. And finally, the book offers fifty exercises for student actors to investigate Brecht's ideas for themselves, becoming thoroughly familiar with the tools in the Brecht toolkit.

Stephen Unwin is one of Britain's leading theatre and opera directors. He worked at the Traverse Theatre in the 1980s, founded English Touring Theatre in 1993, and in 2008 was appointed Artistic Director of the Rose Theatre, Kingston. He has written guides to *Shakespeare's Plays*; *Ibsen, Chekhov and Strindberg*; *Twentieth-Century Drama*; *the Plays of Bertolt Brecht*; and *So You Want To Be A Theatre Director?*

ISBN 978-1-85459-550-8

9 781854 595508 >

THE COMPLETE
STANISLAVSKY
TOOLKIT

Bella Merlin

Also available